Independent Farming: Farming Law – A Guide for Farmers

Willie Penrose B.L., T.D.

First Law

Published in 2006 by
First Law Limited
Merchant's Court,
Merchants Quay,
Dublin 8,
Ireland.

Typeset by Gough Typsetting Services, Dublin.

ISBN 1-904480-55-1

A catalogue record for this book
is available from the British Library.

Printed by
Johnswood Press Ltd.

Introduction

We are all fascinated by the law and by its potential to impinge on our lives, especially in a world where farming has moved from being a simple way of life to being an intricate business full of the legal complexities of property ownership.

This book, which guides readers through the maze of law that now applies to farming, is by no means a dry legal treatise. Yes, it deals comprehensively with the huge body of law that farmers need to be familiar with these days, but it can never be accused of being dull because it livens up its subjects with copious examples of how the law has been applied in practice. The result is an interesting, lively approach to a subject that is all too often presented in a tedious and drab manner. We dare you to be bored by this book!

The author, Willie Penrose, is a distinguished barrister and politician whose work in both Dublin and the midlands has given him an insight into the intricacies of the law as it applies, in particular, to rural Ireland. He is well aware, for instance, that farmers are under increased scrutiny, not only in keeping up with the myriad of regulations they must comply with under EU law but also for the part they play in preserving the environment. Land values are reaching new heights, with farmers being forced to go to some extraordinary lengths to ensure their property is safe from succession and boundary claims. Increased traffic on rural roads and the controversial bid by hill walkers for access to farmland has made liability a crucial issue for every farmer to understand. All these subjects are dealt with here.

Knowledge of the rights and duties of the landowner is essential in an age where so many people are litigious. By reading this book you will become more aware of the constraints the law imposes upon you as a farmer and, more importantly, you will learn how best to protect yourself from the law.

This book is an important reference work for anyone involved in farming today.

Maeve Dineen,
Editor,
Farming Independent.

Preface

As a Dáil Deputy and a Barrister I was motivated to bring this book into existence for one main reason and that is to make the Law more accessible to people. The topic considered in each chapter in this book is the subject matter of countless texts and articles. What I sought to achieve by this book is to provide people with a reference point, whether they have a problem or simply an interest in the area. Each of the chapters contained in the book have been the subject of legal texts which are technical and in most cases aimed at Lawyers. What I hope I have achieved with this text is to give guidance and an understanding of the type of legal issues that arise and the Courts attitude and decisions in these areas. Having spent a number of years working as an agricultural consultant, I encountered a number of issues which were raised on a frequent basis by farmers and which touched upon their responsibilities, duties and obligations from a legal perspective, and I hope that this book will help them in addressing many of the questions that they posed and which exercised their minds, and which I have no doubt continue to do so.

It is, of course, always advisable to consult a Solicitor if you have a legal problem.

I have to admit that there were times when I wondered why I had taken on this project from Bart Daly, but on reflection it has always been my practice as a politician to make myself personally available to people who have difficulties, issues and problems. The provision of understandable and readable legal information is, in my view, the continuation of my view of the role of a politician.

There is no doubt in my mind that without the unique support of Stephen Boggs, Barrister-at-Law, this book would not have seen the light of day. Stephen put his shoulder to the wheel of this project and helped bring it over the line. Oftentimes in the course of my work I hear people complain about the youth. I don't share that view. Stephen Boggs is a shining example of the new generation of Ireland – eager, industrious, bright and enthusiastic. I want to thank him most sincerely for his sterling efforts. I have no doubt he has a bright future in the Law.

Enormous thanks are due to my colleague on the Midland Circuit, Tom Flynn, Barrister-at-Law, for his input, advice and assistance on environmental areas touched on in this text.

I would also like to pay thanks to the officials and staff in the Department of Agriculture and Food at all levels who provided extraordinary help and assistance to me especially in the technical areas surrounding farm entitlements and the control of animal diseases, and in particular Andy McGarrigle and John Moloney. I want to acknowledge their guidance and interest in ensuring that I was kept on the right track in these complex areas.

The Law Library staff at the Four Courts and particularly Des Mulhere at the issue desk for his assistance.

Many colleagues in the Law Library provided encouragement, with some good-humoured ribbing, which made the task easier. My colleagues of the Midland Bar – Colm Smith, S.C., Eddie Walsh, S.C., Fergus O'Hagan, S.C. and Stephen Byrne, B.L. – I thank them too.

It would be remiss of me not to acknowledge the unstinting support and encouragement I receive from my great friends and colleagues Máire Whelan, S.C. and Bernard McCabe, B.L., who have always helped to illuminate the darkest hours especially when Bart Daly was pressing the deadline buttons. They always came to the rescue and I managed to meet these time constraints with literally seconds to spare.

I would also like to thank Ita McAuliffe who has moved

with consummate ease to bring this project to a conclusion.

I would also like to thank Frank Millar of *The Irish Times* for supplying the picture of me used on the back cover

I also wish to thank my mother and father, May Jo and Thomas, and my brothers and sisters who have always stood four square behind me and encouraged me in all the tasks I have undertaken to date.

I would also like to thank my wife, Anne, and my daughters, Aisling, Niamh and Deirdre for their support throughout this and all my other projects. Without their support and understanding it would not be possible to undertake many engagements and projects, such as this, in my public life as a Dáil Deputy and as a Barrister.

W. Penrose, B.L., T.D.

Willie Penrose TD
Spokesperson on Social and Family Affairs

Constituency:
Westmeath
Euro Electoral Region:
East
Electoral Status:
Willie is currently a sitting TD for Westmeath .

Address:
Ballintue
Ballynacargy
Co. Westmeath

Tel:
Home: 044-93-73264
Constituency Office: 044-93-43987
Dáil: 01-6183734
Fax: Dáil: 01-6184541
Fax: Constituency Office: 044-93-43966

Email:
willie.penrose@oireachtas.ie

Political Career:
Chairperson of the Labour Parliamentary Party Chairperson
of Joint Oireachtas Committee on Social and Family Affairs
Member of Westmeath Childcare Committee Labour Party
Spokesperson on Agriculture and Food 1997-2002;

Labour Party Spokesperson on Agriculture and Rural
Development 1992-1997;

First Elected Dáil Éireann 1992;

Former Member Joint Committee on Agriculture, Food and
Rural Development; Member of Westmeath County Council

from 1984 until the ending of the dual mandate in 2003 Former Member of Westmeath Planning and Environmental Committee Former Member An Coiste Gaeilge, Westmeath County Council; Former Chairperson, Labour Party Agricultural Policy and Rural Development Committee.

Occupation:
Full-time Public Representative;
Barrister at Law.

Memberships:
Member, Ballynacargy G.A.A.
Club Member, Cullion Hurling Club
Member, Royal Canal Amenity Group

Family Background:
Married to Anne Fitzsimons, three daughters Ashling, Niamh and Deirdre

Birth Details:
Born in Mullingar, August 1956

Education:
St. Mary's C.B.S. Mullingar; Multyfarnham Agricultural College; University College Dublin; Kings Inns.

Willie started his career in politics when, at just 13, he became the branch secretary in his home town of Ballynacargy.

He was first elected to the Dáil in November 1992, he was re-elected in the 1997 and 2002 General Elections.

In 1984, Willie was elected to Westmeath County Council and remained a member of the local authority until the ending of the dual mandate in 2003.

Since being elected for Labour in the so-called "Spring tide" of 1992, Penrose has continued to be a poll-topper for Labour. Prior to Willie's election, the party had not had a seat in Westmeath since 1927.

He has been described as "a star electoral performer", that defied national trends in 1997 when he topped the poll with 8,037 votes – just 160 short of the quota. His popularity throughout his constituency has been strong since then. In the 1999 local elections, he won more than 42 per cent of the votes in Mullingar West and in 2002 he topped the poll.

To my Parents
May Jo and Thomas

Table of Contents

Table of Cases

W

Table of Legislation

Statutory instruments

European Directives and Regulations

CHAPTER 1

Occupiers Liability

The Occupiers Liability Act 1995 came into force on June 17, 1995 and in so doing substantially changed the law in relation to the control of land in Ireland. The Act largely resulted from the lobbying by parties concerned with the uncertainty that existed in the common law with regard to the liability of parties who were in the occupation of land and for those persons who entered upon that land with or without permission. The Act's substantial impact can be attributed in part to its simplification of the law in relation to the types of person who now constitute entrants on to land.

Three categories of entrant

For the purpose of the legislation there are now three categories of person who enter on to the land of another. Those persons are either:

> (1) A visitor; or
> (2) a recreational user; and finally,
> (3) a trespasser.

What is occupation?

Prior to an examination of the obligations placed on the occupier to each of those three separate categories of persons, it is apt to consider firstly what the definition of occupation is, and secondly what is in fact occupied.

The statutory provision for an occupier is provided at section 1(1) of the Act which reads:

"'Occupier' in relation to any premises means a person exercising such control over the state of the premises, that it is reasonable to impose upon that person a duty towards an entrant in respect of a particular danger thereon and, where there is more than one occupier of the same premises, the extent of the duty of each occupier towards an entrant depends on the degree of control each of them has over the state of the premises and the particular danger thereupon and whether, as respects each of them, the entrant concerned is a visitor, recreational user or trespasser."

The implications that arise from the foregoing are multifold.

Firstly, the definition of an occupier makes no reference to the ownership of the property – rather the person who exercises physical control over the premises is the person upon whom liability under this Act will attach. The element of control is the primary consideration in terms of any one user – occupier and also in terms of any shared responsibility, where multiple parties are said to be in control of premises.

Secondly, the duty only extends to "*state of the premises*", and as such deals with occupancy rather than any activity undertaken by the occupier. So for example, if a gate has been broken and the occupier failed to fix it, is he liable for the fact that somebody walks into the field and is injured by animal who resides therein, or alternatively that the bull in the field with the broken gate escapes and causes harm or damage? The point may seem a fine one, but the High Court had difficulties in refining the issues.[1]

Thirdly, What is required from the Occupier? The Reasonableness test is an objective standard and employed by the courts in coming to conclusions as to what duty the law can impose upon the occupier.

---

[1]   *Smith v. C.I.E.* [1991] I.R. 314.

Finally, those involved in drafting the legislation evidently envisioned multiple occupier liability arising quite frequently, however there is a failure in that legislation to outlining the analysis for the "*degree of control*" – does a two week visit, once per year, constitute occupancy?

What is occupied?

The second major question that falls for analysis, before we approach the question of a duty of care owed to the entrant, is what in fact constitutes a premises? Put it another way – what is occupied?

Section 1(1) of the Act provides that:

> "'*premises*' includes – land, water and any fixed or moveable structures thereupon and also includes vehicles, vessels, trains, aircraft and any other means of transport."

This expansive definition would appear to cover almost all aspects of the modern farm environment.

(i) **Land:**
The land itself would therefore include, forestry, woodlands, bog lands (no reference is made to the purpose or standard required of the land).

(ii) **Water:**
Water would cover moving and still water.

(iii) **Structures:**
It would seem clear from the wording of the legislation that fixed structures thereupon would cover barns, sheds, silos, crushes etc. It more than likely extends to underground

storage of silage and/or slurry.[2] Moveable structures on land would be semi-permanent structures which include cabins, huts, scaffolding, and tree-houses possibly.

(iv) Transport:
The extension of the definition to cover other modes of transport would indicate the duty of the occupying farmer will also extend to farm machinery and equipment for the purposes of the legislation.

So having examined what is occupied and who in fact constitutes an occupier, it is clear that the most important area focused upon under the new legislation is the duty owed to those who enter upon the land in various capacities, either at the occupiers request, with the occupiers consent or permission, either express or implied, and finally those categories of person who enter on to the land without the occupiers permission. Again there are three categories of person each defined by section 1(1) of the 1995 Act.

Category 1: The visitor

A Visitor is a person who is an entrant on the land other than a recreational user who is present on the premises at the invitation or with the permission, of the occupier.

A Visitor is an entrant specified in paragraph (a), (b) or (c) of the definition of "*recreational user*", be an entrant, other than a recreational user, who is present on the premises by virtue of an express or implied term in a contract.

A Visitor is an entrant as of right, this definition of visitor extends to the person while he or she is so present, as the

---

[2] *Mason v. Leavy* [1952] I.R. 40.

case may be, for the purpose for which he or she is invited or permitted to be there:

- for the purpose of the performance of the contract, or
- for the purpose of the exercise of the right,

and this includes any such entrant whose presence on the premises has become unlawful after entry thereon and who is taking reasonable steps to leave.

It should be noted at the outset that the second part of the definition of a visitor extends to cover any person who has been asked to remove themselves from the premises as occupied so that the duty of the occupier to the person who is no longer welcome still extends to that visitor until they have removed themselves from the premises. The use and purpose of this definition is to allow those persons who are:

(i) by right, or
(ii) invited onto, or
(iii) entitled to be upon,

occupied land to give those persons a clear statutory footing.

The duty owed to a visitor

The duty that is owed by the occupier of land to visitors thereon is contained in section 3 of the Occupiers Liability Act 1995. Section 3(1) reads as follows:

"An occupier of a premises owes a duty of care ('the common duty of care') towards a visitor thereto except in so far as the occupier extends, restricts, modifies or excludes that duty in accordance with section 5".

Section 5, which we will look at subsequently, deals with an occupier's entitlement/ability to modify his duty to entrants on to his property. We will look specifically at visitors.

What is the duty of care owed?

Section 3 (2) broadly defines the common duty of care as a duty to take such care as is reasonable in all the circumstances to ensure that a visitor to the premises does not suffer injury or damage by reason of any danger existing thereon.

In effect this is what is known as the reasonable standard of care in tort law.

Visitor's duty of care

It should be noted that the visitor must take reasonable care for his or her own safety, and further that where there are any persons requiring supervision such as children, the extent of control and supervision required when the child is in the company of a person who would normally have control of supervision of that child.

The standard here again is that standard which may be reasonable to expect from that person exercising control or supervision.

The nature and extent of the statutory duty to "visitors", has been expanded upon in a well reasoned judgement delivered by Judge Brian McMahon in the case of *Heaves v. Westmeath County Council*.[3] Indeed Judge McMahon gave very importance guidance on application of the Occupiers Liability Act 1995, in the course of the aforesaid judgement. In this case, the plaintiff was visiting a very well known tourist attraction, at Belvedere House, outside of Mullingar, which is owned by Westmeath County Council. In the course of the visit, he was injured when he slipped on steps when walking

---

[3] Mullingar Circuit Court on October 17, 2001.

on the grounds at Belvedere House with his two children.
Belvedere House had been opened to the public earlier that
summer, and although the house itself was closed on the
particular day that the plaintiff visited the tourist attraction,
nevertheless the gardens and surrounding grounds were open
to visitors, and one can gain access to the various tourist
attractions, by way of steps, which led down from one terrace
down to lower terraces.

It appears that the accident occurred when the plaintiff's
two children had momentarily strayed away from the plaintiff
and he immediately set about looking for them, and in the
course of going down steps, he slipped on an uneven
indentation on the second step which had been partly covered
in moss and was obviously slippy. The plaintiff in the course
of proceedings, argued that Westmeath County Council as
the occupier had breached its common duty of care to him as
a visitor. The plaintiff had driven to the car park where he
had paid an entry fee for himself and indeed also for his two
children. The defendant had people manning the entrance at
the car park for the purpose of effecting the charge. Judge
McMahon in the course of his judgement had no difficulty
characterising the plaintiff as a visitor on the premises for
the purposes of the 1995 Act. He stated:

> "In so far as the term 'visitor' includes an entrant
> who is present on premised by virtue of a contract
> it would seem clear that the Plaintiff in the
> present case should be so classified as a visitor.
> After all, he paid an entry fee in respect of himself
> and his children. At common law he would have
> been classified as a contractual invitee. At
> common law he would also be entitled to
> reasonable care. The history of the legislation in
> question indicates that there was no intention to
> downgrade the legal status of such an entrant.
> The Act was primarily introduced to reverse

McNamara v. E.S.B. [1975] I.R. 1, in respect of trespassers and to create a new category for recreational users who were causing some concern to the agricultural community who feared that the common law might treat them too leniently by according to them the duty of reasonable care.

"Recreational users" on the other hand, was intended to cover people who entered premises with or without permission, without a charge, to engage in a recreational activity conducted in the open air (including any sporting activity), or to engage in scientific research and natural study or to explore caves, visit sites and buildings of historical, architectural, traditional, artistic and archaeological or scientific importance (see section 1(1) of the 1995 Act).

From a careful reading of these definitions, it is clear, that by entering under a contract, the Plaintiff was squarely in the category of visitor and by paying a charge he has held outside the category of recreational user…".

It is apparent from Judge McMahon's judgment, that the Occupiers Liability Act 1995, was clear in declaring that if an entrant comes to the premises under a contract and pays a charge, he is a visitor and only a visitor. It is important to note that in this legislative classification that there are three and only three categories and that these categories are exhaustive and there are no more categories. Furthermore it is equally important to realise that an entrant cannot be in two categories at the same time.

In this case, therefore, the question produced itself as to whether the defendant (Westmeath County Council) had discharged its duty under section 1(1) of the 1995 Act, which was:

> "to take such care as is reasonable in all circumstances (having regard to the care which the visitor may reasonably be expected to take for his own safety and, if the visitor is on the premises in the company of another person, the extent of the supervision and control of the latter person may reasonably be expected to exercise over the visitor's activities), to ensure that a visitor to the premises does not suffer injury or damage by reason of any danger existing thereon".

In this case, the plaintiff's engineer in the course of evidence had pointed out that the step on which the plaintiff had slipped had a rough indentation. He considered that when this was covered with moss it would constitute a trap, and he suggested that the steps might have been cordoned off or that a warning notice might have been placed at the head of the steps so as to alert visitors, or that something in the nature of a hand rail might have been constructed to assist them in going down the steps.

Judge McMahon emphasised that the duty imposed by section 3(1) was one of "*reasonable care and no more*", and he concluded on that basis that the precautions the Defendant had taken, in his view and in all of the circumstances, were reasonable. They had appointed personnel to address the risk, and the head gardener had a satisfactory cleaning system in place that he had brought in for a number of years without encountering any major difficulty or problem. Further, in regard to this particular issue where the gardener had lacked confidence concerning these types of matters, he had recognised his own limitations and engaged an outside expert to advise him and had faithfully implemented the advice he received.

Reducing exposure

As noted above section 5(2)(a) of the Act reads as follows:

> "Subject to this section and to section 8, an occupier may by express agreement or notice restrict, modify or exclude his or her duty towards visitors under section 3"

Section 5(2)(b) reads:

> "Such a restriction, modification or exclusion shall not bind a visitor unless
> – it is reasonable in all the circumstances,
> – in case the occupier purports by notice to so restrict, modify or exclude that duty, the occupier has reasonable steps to bring the notice to the attention of the visitor".

Again at section 5(3) this ability to modify and occupiers duty to a visitor is itself restricted where the Act states at section 3:

> "In respect of a danger existing on premises, a restriction, modification or exclusion referred to in subsection 2, shall not be taken as allowing an occupier to injure a visitor or damage the property of a visitor intentionally or to act with reckless disregard for a visitor or the property of a visitor.

In summary therefore:

> (1) A visitor is required to take precautions and responsibility in regard to his or her own safety when entering an occupied premises.
> (2) An occupier has a duty to a visitor to ensure

that the visitor does not suffer any injury or damage by reason of any danger that exists upon the land. In that regard the standard required of the occupier is that care which is reasonable in all the circumstances. This standard is at the higher end of the spectrum in terms of occupier's liability.

(3) The modification contained in section 5 of the Act at subsection 3 therein, even if employed by the occupier, does not entitle them to reduce their standard and duty of care below that which is owed to a recreational user or to a trespasser. In that regard, the occupier may in effect never act intentionally or with a reckless disregard to injure or damage the property of an entrant on to the land as occupied.

Category 2: The recreational user

Given that the statutory definition of visitor makes express reference to "*recreational user*" it is to this category of person/ entrant to whom we now turn our attention.

Section 1(1) provides that a "*recreational user*" means:

> "an entrant who, with or without the occupiers permission or at the occupiers implied invitation, is present on the premises without a charge being imposed for the purpose of engaging in a recreational activity."

This includes an entrant admitted without charge to a national monument. But excludes an entrant who is present as:

(a) a member of the occupiers family ordinarily resident on the premises;

(b) an entrant who is present at the express invitation of the occupier or such a member of the occupiers family, and

(c) an entrant who is present with the permission of the occupier or such a member for social reasons connected with the occupier or such a member.

What is a recreational activity?

It is to be noted immediately that the definition of recreational activity is extremely broad and as such covers a multitude of activities which may take place.

Recreational activity is defined as any recreational activity conducted, whether alone or with others:

– in the open air (including any sporting activity),

– scientific research and nature studies so conducted,

– exploring caves, and

– visiting sites and buildings of historical, architectural, traditional, artistic, archaeological or of scientific importance.

The first point to be made is that where a charge exists in relation to land, that person cannot be said to be a recreational user, therefore public amenities that charge for the purposes of entrants cannot be said to have a recreational use. They fall into the first category and the persons who engage in visiting those sites and who pay for the privilege of doing so must fall into the category of visitor.

The second point, it is assumed (subject to any judicial clarification) that the phrase any sporting activity includes hill walking, hiking, mountain climbing and other activities, which have in the past proved somewhat contentious with occupiers of land.

It is also assumed that the sites and buildings described for the purposes of being of historical, architectural, traditional, artistic, archaeological or of scientific importance would also mean that urban occupiers will face challenges here.

Obviously a question arises as to the scope of the definition of recreational user and how it can be applied, for example, to children who engage in what are no doubt, in ordinary language, recreational activities such as playing soccer or Gaelic football in the school grounds, where they would be entitled to do so by the very fact that there is a connection between them and the occupier, as this is also the place of their educational establishment.

Professor William Binchy, one of the authors of *Irish Tort Law*,[4] an authoritive book in this area in Ireland, has indicated that people who are at school who kick a ball around the yard before school opens would normally be considered visitors rather than recreational users, but if they do so at a time earlier than that has been permitted by the school, their status is less clear. Likewise he noted that if they turned up at the playground at the week-end or in the middle of summer holidays, at a point at which their ancillary relationship fades into the background and the prospect of their being characterised as recreational users, or indeed trespassers, is not easy to identify.

Likewise Professor Binchy pointed out in a paper given at the School of Law, Trinity College, Dublin, dealing with the recent developments in tort law,[5] that similar difficulties could arise in relation to public car parks and other open

---

[4] McMahon and Binchy *Irish Tort Law* (Dublin, Butterworths).
[5] Torts 2002 Conference, School of Law, Trinity College, Dublin, Friday, July 19, 2002.

areas. He illustrated this by reference to the case of *Byrne v. Dun Laoghaire/Rathdown County Council*.[6] The plaintiff was an adult who fell when training an under fifteen soccer team at the playing fields in Sallynoggin, County Dublin, at the end of July. The defendant had contended that the plaintiff had not received its permission to use the playing fields at this time as it was off season. Mr. Justice Smith held that he was a recreational user and he acquitted the defendant of liability in respect of the indentation (rather than hole), in the ground where the plaintiff fell. Professor Binchy concluded that:

> "One can understand the Court's treating the use of areas specifically devoted to team games as falling under the distinctive rules involving a separation between visitors and recreational users, as otherwise there would be no orderly management of the use of these area for the benefits of all".

What duty is owed to recreational users?

Section 4 of the 1995 Act, outlines the duty, which is owed by occupiers to recreational users in the following terms: occupiers owe a duty:

(1) not to injure the person or damage the property of the person intentionally, and
(2) occupiers must not act with reckless disregard for the person or the property of that person.

---

[6] 20 I.R. LT(ns) 16, a Circuit Court case heard by the then President, Mr. Justice Esmond Smith, November 13, 2001.

Section 4(2) of the Act provides a wide list of factors which aid the Court and the occupier in determining what will constitute reckless disregard for the person.

i.   Did the occupier know, did the occupier have a reasonable ground for belief that a danger existed on the premises?

ii. Was the occupier aware or should the occupier have been aware that the person was on the premises?

iii. Did the occupier know that the person so on the premises was in the near vicinity of the danger which existed upon the premises?

iv. Was the danger one which the occupier might reasonably have been expected to provide protection from?

v.   How onerous would the burden of removing the danger or of protecting the person have been? Regard is to be had here for factors such as difficulty, expense and impracticability, having regard to the character of the premises and the degree of danger of so doing.

vi. Is the character of the premises conducive to recreational activity?

vii. The occupier may also have regard to the conduct of the person whether or not he or she acted reasonably in taking care for their own safety while on the premises.

viii.Was any warning given by the occupier or any other person to the recreational user of the danger which may have or indeed did exist thereupon?

Significant guidance as to the scope and extent of this

definition can be found in a Supreme Court decision in the
case of *Weir-Rodgers v. S.F. Trust Ltd.*[7]

The case itself involved a plaintiff who had slipped from
a beauty spot and had fallen some substantial distance to the
sea beneath.

Essentially the argument alleged against the defendant
was two-fold. It was suggested the area should have been
fenced so as to prevent anybody entering on to it and
additionally or alternatively, there should have been a warning
notice. At the trial in the High Court the judge held against
the plaintiff on the first ground but held with the plaintiff on
the second ground. Several aspects of the case are pertinent
here. The Supreme Court held that:

> "it is perfectly obvious to all users of land higher
> than sea level but adjoining the sea there may
> well be a dangerous cliff and in those
> circumstances the occupier of lands cannot be
> held unreasonable in not putting up a warning
> notice".

The net effect of this and the consideration of English
jurisprudence is that the *common sense expectation* of persons
engaged in outdoor activities such as, for instance, mountain
climbing or walking or swimming in dangerous areas is taken
seriously into account by the Court and the concept of
common sense and personal responsibility is much to the fore.

The other side of that coin is that the occupier is entitled
to assume that knowledge of such dangers and risk would
exist and safety measures would be taken.

Further the Court endorsed the idea that risks attaching
to beauty spots and other municipal facilities are risks "*just
one of the results of the world as we find it*". Following that
rationale, Geoghegan J. concluded that:

---

[7]   [2005] 1 I.R. 43, 53.

> "the person sitting down near a cliff must be
> prepared for oddities in the cliffs structure or in
> the structure of the ground adjacent to the cliff
> and he or she assumes the inherent risk associated
> therewith".

The result of this passage must surely copper fasten the
position of the occupier in terms of recreational users wherein
objective criteria in terms of common sense are employed. It
is appropriate to note that:

> "there could, of course, be something quite
> exceptionally unusual and dangerous in the state
> of a particular piece of ground which would
> impose a duty on the occupier the effect of which
> would be that if he did not put up a warning notice
> he would be treated as having reckless disregard.
> It is therefore clear if the normal situation exists
> and people are to have regard for their own safety
> using a reasonable standard of common sense
> wherein natural threats or risks are to be
> encountered while enjoying the status of
> recreational user, then those recreational users
> must carry the burden of such risks. However,
> wherein exceptional or unforeseen risks are
> involved, those who have substantial or
> particularised or specialised knowledge of any
> such risk and who are also in occupation of the
> land whereupon that risks exists, must attempt
> and/or endeavour to ensure people are adequately
> warned and/or given adequate notice of the
> existence of such risk".

This helpful elucidation of the duty imposed upon recreational
users, and the countervailing obligations on the occupier of
the land are heavily reliant upon a rational person exercising

common sense and taking cognisance of the nature of the land that they have entered upon for their recreation.

Category 3: The trespasser

The third category of person to whom a duty is owed by an occupier is a trespasser. A trespasser is defined under the legislation as an entrant other than a recreational user or a visitor. The duty which is owed to a trespasser is exactly that as provided for a recreational user already.

The duty owed to a trespasser

Section 4(1) of the Act reads:

> "in respect of a danger existing on a premises, an occupier owes towards a recreational user of the premises or a trespasser thereupon, a duty (a) not to injure the person or damage the property of the person intentionally, and (b) not to act with reckless disregard for the person or the property of the person".

However, section 4(3) provides:

> "where a person enters on to premises for the purpose of committing an offence, or, while present thereon, commits an offence, the occupier shall not be liable for a breach of the duty imposed by section 1(b) unless a Court determines otherwise in the interests of justice".

It is, as yet, unascertained in what manner the Courts will exercise this discretion.

The duty which is owed to a trespasser is not to intentionally injure that person. However, section 57(1) of the Civil Liability Act 1961, coupled with section 8(a) of the Occupiers Liability Act 1995, has resonance in recent public outcries which have focused upon the right to use reasonable or proportionate force to defend one's property:

> "nothing in this Act shall be construed as affecting any enactment or any rule of law relating to self defence, the defence of others or the defence of property to whit an occupier is entitled to use "proportionate" force in the defence of his or her property or his or her self therefore one may protect oneself and one's property from any person intent upon depriving the owner of said property".

The usefulness of this defence of proportionate force as a defence or protection of one's property has been the subject of considerable comment in the wake of the case involving *DPP v. Padraig Nally* who was convicted of manslaughter[8] and he was sentenced to 6 years.[9] Following this conviction there have been demands to change the law, culminating in Bills being introduced in Seanad Éireann and Dáil Éireann, seeking extra protection for homeowners who are confronted by burglars. The argument put forward is that homeowners do not have the absolute right to defend themselves, when an intruder enters, as the law is open to interpretation.

The Non-Fatal Offences Against the Person Act 1997, allows the use of force "only such as is reasonable in the circumstances" for a person to protect themselves or members of their family from injury, assault or detention caused by a criminal act. The use of force in these circumstances can be as reasonable as the person applying the force, believes it to

---

[8] Unreported, Central Criminal Court sitting at Castlebar, County Mayo, July 12, 2005.
[9] Unreported, Central Criminal Court in Dublin, November 11, 2005.

be. Therefore the whole issue of self defence boils down to the question of whether the force was reasonable. Of course, there can be no precise answer available to this question of what is reasonable force, since no two sets of circumstances can ever be precisely the same.

It appears that the issue of the protection of homeowners is one that will be the subject of further legislative intervention in the not too distance future.

CHAPTER 2

Succession

There are a number of clear objectives in this chapter, which are central to ensuring that assets of an agricultural nature are disposed of in an orderly fashion. In summary those are:

Firstly, to explain the purpose of drawing up and ensuring a valid will exists upon the death of an asset owner.

Secondly, to inform those who remain after the death of a relative of their rights and entitlements. And in particular the rights and entitlements of spouses and children, and finally to provide for some basic guidelines in relation to intestacy, i.e. where no will has been prepared.

As a preliminary note, this chapter should not be taken as a substitute for a consultation with a legal professional in relation to instructions, wishes or intentions which are to be carried out after a person dies. There is no substitute as effective or as trouble-free as the effective and clear execution of a will under the supervision of a competent and qualified legal professional. When a person dies having made such a will which disposes of all of his or her worldly goods and possession, that person is said to have died testate. The ambulatory nature of the document ensures that it takes no effect until the party who executed it, i.e. the testator, has passed on.

Testamentary capacity

Section 77 of the Succession Act 1965, provides that section 77(1) therein, to be valid a will shall be made by a person who –

"(a) Has attained the age of eighteen years, or is
     or has been married, and
(b) is of sound disposing mind."

On foot of section 77(2) a person who is entitled to appoint a
guardian of an infant may make the appointment by will
notwithstanding he is not a person to whom section 77(1)(a)
applies.

The test in effect means that a presumption exists that the
person is of sound mind, where the will appears to be to all
intents and purposes rational, however, as always where
mental capacity of the testator is open to challenge or even
where a perception exists that the testators capacity could be
open to challenge, an affidavit verifying the capacity of the
testator could and should be obtained from the testators
medical personnel by the solicitor responsible for the drafting
of the will. In effect the test has grown up in Ireland that: -

(1) the testator must know the extent of his
    estate;
(2) the testator must understand that he is
    drawing up a will in order to dispose of his
    estate upon his death, and
(3) the testator must also be able to call to mind
    those persons due to benefit from any
    bequeath under the will.

Further it is to be noted that the Court has an inherent
jurisdiction derived from the Courts of Equity prior to 1877,
to refuse a grant of probate of a will if the Court is not satisfied
that the will was the free and intelligent act of the testator. It
is important to remember that the onus of proof in deciding
whether or not the testator had the capacity to make a will
rests upon the person who is endorsing or promoting the will.

Formalities

These are contained in section 78 of the Succession Act 1965, which sets out the formalities that must be undertaken and accurately completed in order for the will to have legal effect. Section 78 reads as follows:

> "To be valid a will shall be in writing and be executed in accordance with the following rules:
>
> (1) It shall be signed at the foot or end thereof by the testator, or by some person in his presence and by his direction.
>
> (2) Such signature shall be made or acknowledged by the testator in the presence of each of two or more witnesses, present at the same time, and each witness shall attest by his signature the signature of the testator in the presence of the testator, but no form of attestation shall be necessary nor shall it be necessary for the witnesses to sign in the presence of each other.
>
> (3) So far as concerns the position of the signature of the testator or of the person signing for him under rule 1, it is sufficient if the signature is so placed at or after, or following, or under, or beside, or opposite to the end of the will that it is apparent on the face of the will that the testator intended to give effect by signature to the writing signed as his will.
>
> (4) Under subsection 4 no such will shall be affected by the circumstances – (a) that the signature does not follow or is not immediately after the foot or end of the will; or (b) that a blank space intervenes between the concluding word of the will and the

signature; or (c) that the signature is placed
among the words of the testimonium clause
or of the clause of attestation, or follows or
is after or under the clause of attestation,
either with or without a blank space
intervening, or follows or is after, or under,
or beside the names of one of the names of
the attesting witnesses; or (d) that the
signature is on a side or page or other portion
of the paper or papers containing the will on
which no clause or paragraph or disposing
part of the will is written above the signature;
or (e) that there appears to be sufficient space
on or at the bottom of the preceding side or
page or other portion of the same paper on
which the will is written to contain the
signature; and the enumeration of the above
circumstances shall not restrict the generality
of rule 1.

(5) The signature shall not be operative to give
effect to any disposition or direction inserted
after the signature is made."

We will come back to points (4) and (5) which deal with the
importance of the signature, however, subsections (1), (2)
and (3) deal with equally important areas.

Subsection 1 requires that the will must be in writing
which gives rise to the issues which related to and surround
the use of on-line or digital formatting for wills and also in
relation to the use of word processors for the printing of wills,
the main problem with which is that, will were historically
deemed to be continuous documents. Where such equipment
is to be used it should be made clear from the face of the
document that same has been used that when the will has
been attested and sworn it should be made clear the number

of pages and the fact that only one side of each page has been used.[1]

Section 78 (2) deals with the issues of witnesses to a will and the signature thereupon and made by the testator in the presence of same. The upshot of Rule 2 is that both witnesses must be present at the same time when they witness the making of the signature or acknowledge the making of the signature by the testator. However, they do not need to be present when the testator signs the will as long as they are both present together when the testator acknowledges the signature. Finally, they need not both be present simultaneously when they sign the will as the witnesses, although each must sign in the presence of the testator. Further it is to be noted in terms of Rule 2 that no particular phrase of attestation need be used.

The signature of the witnesses attest to the signature of the testator and not of the will itself. There is absolutely no requirement that the witnesses must have read and/or have any knowledge of the will whatsoever. The role of the witness is to attest to the signature of the testator or testatrix on the document. Failing to adequately use a simple attestation clause could result in unnecessary difficulties subsequently.

In terms of witnesses we have already seen that the witnesses need not sign in the presence of each other nor must they witness the contents of the document. However, there are some stipulations in relation to witnesses that should be noted at this juncture. Firstly, under section 82(1) of the Succession Act 1965, any person who attests to the execution of a will, and if any devise, bequest, estate, interest, gift or appointment of or affecting any property given under that will to that witness or to that witness's spouse shall be utterly null and void. It is strongly recommended therefore that any party who stands to benefit in any way whatsoever or whose

---

[1]   See Spierin, *Wills Irish Precedence and Drafting* (Dublin, 1999).

spouse may stand to benefit in any way whatsoever should under no circumstances attest to or be a witness to any will or document relating thereto.

Regarding the location of the signature of the testator or the person signing on his behalf under Rule 1, those Rules are subsequently strengthened by Rules 4 and 5 that exist under the Act, which deal with the location of the signature on or about the face of the will. Some latitude will be afforded if the intention of the testator to execute the will can be established. However for clarity sake, the position of the signature must be found at the end or foot of the will. Again best practice is to follow conventional wisdom and to ensure that signature is placed at the foot of or end of or immediately after the text of the will. However, as already stated, latitude will be afforded in order to give effect to the expressed intentions of the deceased.

Although those formal requirements as listed above may seem trite, academic or outdated, they are not to be taken lightly and the proviso in relation to wills as stated above, namely that they should be drafted by an adequately trained legal professional, should not be overlooked. These technicalities have developed centuries. It can be all traced to logical rules which by and large have the intention of giving effect to the wishes of the testator.

Amending the will

Section 86 of the Succession Act 1965, provides:

> "An obliteration, interlineation, or any other alteration made in a will after execution shall not be valid or have any effect, unless such alteration is executed as is required for the execution of the will; but the will, with such alteration as part thereof, shall be deemed to be duly executed if the signature of the testator and

the signature of each witness is made in the margin or on some other part of the will opposite or near to such alteration, or at the foot or end of or opposite to a memorandum referring to such alteration, and written at the end of some other part of the will".

It is clear from this that any alterations made to the will must be witnessed by the same witnesses who must also sign that they have witnessed the testator making the same alteration after the testator has also signed the same alteration.

In terms of revoking a will, there are several ways in which a party may revoke a will under the Succession Act 1965.

Method 1:
Section 85(2), provides a will may be revoked by a *later will*. To that effect the phrase "I hereby revoke all former wills" is usually inserted at the beginning of each and every will.

Method 2:
Section 85(2), further provides that a will may be revoked by *burning, tearing or destruction of it* by the testator or by some person in his presence and by his direction with the intention of revoking it. It is clear from this that the destruction requires a *mens rea* and an *actus reus*.

Method 3:
Section 85(1) provides that a will is automatically revoked by the subsequent marriage of the testator. However any will made in contemplation of that marriage will not be revoked whether it is expressly stated and set out in the will or not.

Where a will is missing upon the death of the testator a

presumption exists at law that the will was destroyed by him and the intention of the testator is presumed to be that he intended to revoke the said will. This presumption is open to being rebutted by evidence to the contrary.

Proving the will

Section 90 of the Succession Act 1965, altered the law to allow for extrinsic evidence to be admitted to show the intention of the testator, and secondly to assist in the construction of or to explain any contradiction within a will. This is an exception to the rules that extrinsic or external evidence is not normally admissible. Such evidence will only be admitted where the will is unclear.

If, as in the case of *Rowe v. Law*[2] wherein the Supreme Court held that the intention of the testator was clear, no extrinsic evidence will be allowed to aid in the interpretation or construction of the will.

After the death of the testator

At this point it may be appropriate to provide a brief summary of the procedure which follows up to and including and post the grant of probate in relation to a will.

It is the norm for the testator or testatrix to nominate an executor to perform the functions associated with the distribution of assets under a will.

Once that person extracts a grant of probate, then that person becomes fixed with the duties and liabilities attached to that of an executor from which he cannot resile.

Functions of the executor

The main functions and tasks to be performed by an executor are:-

---

[2]   [1978] I.R. 55.

(1) to enumerate all assets,

(2) to discharge any liabilities attaching to the estate, and

(3) to administer the remainder of the estate pursuant to the wishes of the testator once payment and debts and liabilities have been discharged by the executor.

The Executor is then bound to administer the remainder of the estate in accordance with the terms and conditions of the will. It is to be noted that the High Court has sole and exclusive jurisdiction to issue and revoke grants of probate. This jurisdiction is most commonly and regularly exercised by the Probate Office and the District Probate Registries which are both functions of the High Court.

In effect that brings us to the end of testacy where a will has been properly created and a grant of probate has been taken out and the will is adequately administered pursuant to its terms by an executor.

It should be noted at this point that there is a presumption of due execution with the statutory formalities and anyone who wishes to challenge those in terms of accuracy and/or compliance assumes the burden of proof which in effect means they must establish that either formalities were incorrectly complied with or not complied with at all.

Freedom of Testation

A person who wishes to make a will must recognise this is made under the restrictions upon the freedom of testation which exist.

Pursuant to sections 111, 112 and 117 of the 1965 Act, there are several restrictions upon the freedom of the testator to leave both his real and personal property to persons other than his surviving spouse and/or issue. These are known as the legal rights of the testator's spouse and the legal requirement for the testator/testatrix to provide for his children.

Legal rights of the surviving spouse

Section 111 reads:

> "if the testator leaves a spouse and no children,
> the spouse shall have a right to one half of the
> estate".

If the testator leaves a spouse and children then the spouse shall have a right to one-third of the estate. The right of a spouse is known as a legal right share and takes priority over devises and bequests in a will which shares upon partial testacy.

It is to be further noted here that section 115 of the Act provides where a person dies entirely testate, a spouse has the right to elect between the legacy in the will and what is known as the legal rights share as described pursuant to section 111. Where a spouse fails to obtain any benefit at all under a will there is no necessity for that spouse to make an election pursuant to section 115 as they are automatically entitled to their legal rights share.

Joint bank accounts

Section 4(3) of the Succession Act 1965 provides-

> "For the purposes of this Act—
> (c) the estate or interest of a deceased person
>   under a joint tenancy where any tenant
>   survives the deceased person shall be deemed
>   to be an estate or interest ceasing on his
>   death."

Inter alia, this in effect means that the survivor takes the funds remaining in a joint bank account in the absence of any contrary intention of the deceased.

Entitlements of surviving children

Section 117 of the Succession Act 1965 attempt to ensure that proper provision is made for children under any such will.

The distinction here, however, is immediately apparent as the obligation is upon the child to apply to the Court for a ruling that the testator has failed to make proper provision for that child within the testator's means.

A wide discretion is then afforded to the Court once it is satisfied that proper provision has not been made to order any provision it sees fit to be made for the child out of the estate.

In exercising this discretion the Court lends its mind to the point of view of a prudent and just parent:

> "taking into account the position of each of the children of the testator and any other circumstances".

Obviously both of these provisions only apply where the party dies testate or partially testate.

It is important to note that the provision contained in section 117 is not a legal right, as such. As such any award made by a court under section 117 cannot affect the rights and entitlements of the surviving spouse.

Time limits

It is also to be noted that the time limitations provided for section 117 would seem to make it very unfair in that the child must apply within six months of the first raising of representation to the estate of the deceased. That affords the child a limited opportunity to seek to have provision made for him or herself.

Onus of proof

Again, a claimant claiming pursuant to section 117 has a "relatively high onus of proof". The test as outlined is as follows: firstly, the Court must decide whether or not the testator has indeed failed in his moral duty to make proper provision for a child, and the second leg of the test goes on to provide that only in the event that he has failed to make such proper provision will the Court decided what, if any, provision is to be ordered to be for that child. It follows therefore that if the child of the testator fails to pass first leg of the test the second leg falls.

It is proposed at this juncture, to elucidate what moral duty and proper provision and moral obligation are judicially interpreted to mean. Such is the body of case law in this area that adequate legal advice should be sought if such an issue arises.

The decision of the High Court of Mr. Justice Kearns in the case of *ABC (deceased)*[3] provides the following list of factors to which a Court will give consideration in an application of this sort. Those factors are:-

> "(a) The social policy underlying section 117 is primarily directed to protecting those children who are still of an age and situation in life where they might reasonably expect support from their parents against the failure of parents, who are unmindful of their duties in that area.
>
> (b) What has to be determined is whether the

---

[3] *In The Estate Of ABC deceased*, unreported, High Court, April 2, 2003.

testator, at the time of his death, owes any moral obligation to the applicants and if so, whether he has failed in that obligation.

(c) There is a high onus of proof placed on an applicant for relief order section 117 which requires the establishment of a positive failure in moral duty

(d) Before a court can interfere there must be clear circumstances and a positive failure in moral duty must be established.

(e) The duty created by section 117 is not absolute.

(f) The relationship of parent and child does not itself and without regard to other circumstances create a moral duty to leave anything by will to the child.

(g) Section 117 does not create an obligation to leave something to each child.

(h) The provision of an expensive education for a child may discharge the moral duty as may other gifts or settlements made during the lifetime of the testator.

(i) Financing a good education so as to give a child the best start in life possible, and providing money, which if properly managed, should afford a degree of financial security for the rest of one's life does amount to making "proper provision".

(j) The duty under section 117 is not to make adequate provision but to provide proper provision in accordance with the testator's means.

(k) A just parent must take into account not just his moral obligations to his children and to his wife, but all his moral obligations, e.g. to aged and infirm parents.

(l) In dealing with a section 117 application, the
     position of an applicant child is not to be
     taken in isolation. The court's duty is to
     consider the entirety of the testator's affairs
     and to decide upon the application in the
     overall context. In other words, while the
     moral claim of a child may require a testator
     to make a particular provision for him, the
     moral claims of others may require such
     provision to be reduced or omitted altogether.

(m) Special circumstances giving rise to a moral
     duty may arise if a child is induced to believe
     that by, for example, working on a farm he
     will ultimately become the owner of it
     thereby causing him to shape his upbringing,
     training and life accordingly.

(n) Another example of special circumstances
     might be a child who had a long illness or an
     exceptional talent which it would be morally
     wrong not to foster.

(o) Special needs would also include physical
     or mental disability.

(p) Although the court has very wide powers
     both as to when to make provisions for an
     applicant child and as to the nature of such
     provision such powers must not be construed
     as giving the court a power to make a new
     will for the testator.

(q) The test to be applied is not which of the
     alternative courses open to the testator the
     court itself would have adopted if confronted
     with the same situation but rather, whether
     the decision of the testator to opt for the
     course he did, of itself and without more,
     constituted a breach of moral duty to the
     plaintiff.

(r) The court must not disregard the fact that parents must be presumed to know their children better than anyone else."

Intestacy

The next section of this chapter will deal substantively with the issues which arise, where there is no will created at all.

Where no will is in fact created at all, intestacy occurs. In the event of this situation arising, there are rules for the distribution of any assets that remain throughout the relative next of kin in order in which they occur and in their priority. Again the Succession Act 1965, provide us with detailed guidelines as to how upon intestacy the estate is to be divided or sub-divided between any and all relevant parties. The matter has been substantially complicated by the Status of Children Act 1987, which provides, *inter alia*, substantive provisions for the children or issue of any relationship held by the testator (more on that later).

Summary of rules upon intestacy

- Pursuant to section 6(1) of the Succession Act 1965, where the intestate leaves *a spouse but no issue surviving* the spouse is entitled to the whole of the estate.
- If there are *a spouse and issue surviving*, the spouse takes two-thirds of the estate, the remaining one-third is distributed amongst the issue,
- If the intestate leaves *issue but no spouse surviving*, the issue then share equally once they are in equal degrees of relationship. It should be noted at this point that section 3(3), of the Succession Act 1965, provided for

what is known as per stirpes distribution of wealth. Put at its simplest, the assets are divided on a percentage basis and calculated relative to the proximity of the relationship to the deceased.

It falls to be noted at this point the distinction that arises after June 14, 1988, the importance of that date is that the Status of Children Act 1987 came into effect. From that point for non-marital children are regarded as issue for the purposes of the distribution of assets upon intestacy. The position is, that after 1988 that non-marital children, if same exist, are entitled to an equal share equivalent to that of marital children. When applying this to our second category where we have a spouse and issue remaining, the spouse will still receive two-thirds of the estate, the children one-third to be divided equally between them regardless of whether or not they were born within the marriage or outside of the marriage.

• Equally in our third category where *issue and no spouse remain*, the total estate is to be divided amongst all issue and that is to include non-marital children.

Who is a spouse?

It is to be noted at this juncture that the Act contains no definition of spouse or issue. A spouse is loosely legally defined as somebody validly married to the intestate. Therefore, any party who has availed themselves of a divorce pursuant to the Divorce Act 1996, will not be entitled to a share in the estate unless they can establish that the terms of their separation and divorce did not make adequate provision for them from marital assets.

Who are issue?

Issue is further not defined within the terms of the Succession Act 1965. Pursuant to the terms of the Status of Children Act 1987, it is to encompass and include both legitimate and illegitimate children, however, there is some dispute as to whether or not the definition will in fact extend to step-children. Further on this point it is to be noted, issue probably does not cover adopted children within the meaning of the Succession Act 1965. That is not to say, however, that adequate provision is not made in the law for adopted children who hold the same property and succession rights after their adoption as any children born to the adoptive parents within wedlock under the Adoption Act 1954.

- Where *no issue and no spouse surviving* at the time of the death of the testator, section 68 of the Succession Act 1965, provides that the parents of the testator, if they are still alive, are entitled to inherit in equal shares. If only one remain, that parent is entitled to the full share of the assets. However it is to be noted that the claim of any illegitimate child will trump that of either parent.

  The immediate family who follow after spouse, issue, and parents is that of brothers and sisters.
- If *no spouse, issue or parents surviving* to inherit the brothers and sisters will again share equally in any assets that exist.
- The penultimate category party entitled to inherit where *no spouse, issue, parents, brothers or sisters* exist is dealt with at

section 70 of the Succession Act 1965. Those are the shares of the next of kin. Section 70(1), reads as follows:-

"If an intestate dies leaving neither spouse nor issue nor parent nor brother nor sister nor children of any deceased of any brother or sister, his estate, shall subject to the succeeding provisions of this part, be distributed in equal shares among his next of kin".

Who are the next of kin?

Section 71 of the Act provided that the person or persons who are at the date of death of the intestate stand nearest in blood relationship to him shall be taken to be his next of kin.

Calculating the definition and degree of blood relationship is a complicated affair and is provided at section 71(2). For the sake of completeness, section 71(2) details the method of computation and reads as follows:-

"Degrees of blood relationship of a direct lineal ancestor shall be computed by counting upwards from the intestate to that ancestor and degrees of blood relationship of any other relative shall be ascertained by counting upwards from the intestate to the nearest ancestor common to the intestate and that relative, and then downward from that ancestor to the relative, but, where a direct lineal ancestor and any other relative are so ascertained to be within the same degree of blood relationship to the intestate, the other relatives shall be preferred to the exclusion of the direct lineal ancestor".

The application of this section, although it seems quite

complicated, may be clarified through the use of an example.
The effect of the rules is as follows if an intestate:

> Mr. X dies leaving only an aunt and a
> grandmother, the grandmother will take to the
> exclusion of the aunt.
>
> Counting up to the grandmother gives us two
> degrees of separation in the relationship, whereas
> to reach the aunt it is necessary to count up from
> Mr. X's mother and then to the grandmother, who
> is the common ancestor as referred to in the
> legislation. One must then count downwards to
> the aunt which is a further step in the separation
> of our relationship between Mr. X and the aunt
> of the intestate. In complicated situations such
> as these, unequal degrees of relationship will be
> sufficient to trump the interest of one party over
> another provided they can prove such separation.
> If the degrees of separation are proved to be
> equal, the rule prefers the younger generation so
> as between the aunt and the great-grandmother
> who are all three degrees of separation from the
> intestate, the aunt would be preferred.

The State's entitlement

Ultimately if none of the above options are available, the
State pursuant to section 73(1) of the Succession Act,
becomes the ultimate "intestate successor". It is to be noted
at this juncture that contains only a summary of the provisions
of the Succession Act 1965, and has quite obviously omitted
the more onerous and complex questions which may arise in
terms of indirect lineage, half-blood, adoption and so on and
so forth.

CHAPTER 3

The Single Payment Scheme

Background

The European Commission's proposals for the Mid-Term Review of the CAP Agenda 2000 were the subject of negotiation for almost a year. Outline proposals were published in July 2002 and the more detailed proposals were published in January 2003. The proposals comprised the most radical reform of the CAP since its foundation and have been the subject of detailed analysis and intense public debate both here and throughout Europe.

The final outcome agreed in the Council of Ministers in Luxembourg on June 26, 2003 contained substantial modifications to the Commission's original proposals and represented an agreement that was balanced between the varying interests of the Member States. It was also a successful outcome from Ireland's point of view. The agreement will reshape the Common Agricultural Policy and secure its future by making it more relevant to modern society and to consumer demands.

The Single Payment Scheme

Following publication of the EU Council Regulation 1782/2003 in September 2003 and having regard to the outcome of consultations with farmers and other interested parties, Ireland decided that the Livestock Premia and Arable Aid Schemes would be fully decoupled from production with effect from January 1, 2005.

The Premia Schemes decoupled from production were:

special Beef Premium, 1st and 2nd age animals; Special Beef Premium – Bulls; Suckler Cow Premium Scheme; Ewe Premium Scheme; Supplementary Ewe Premium (Rural World); Slaughter Premium Scheme; Extensification Premium; National Envelope Top-Ups relating to the Ewe Premium, Dry Heifer, Calved Heifer and Slaughtered Heifers; the Arable Aid Scheme.

The new Single Payment Scheme replaced all of these schemes and was introduced in Ireland in 2005. In addition, a new Dairy Premium was introduced for the first time in 2004. It was coupled with milk production in 2004 (based on milk quota held at March 31, 2004) but was decoupled from milk production in 2005 (based on milk quota held on March 31, 2005) and added to the existing Single Payment Scheme.

Who benefits from the Single Payment Scheme?

In general, the Single Payment Scheme is applicable to farmers who actively farmed during the reference years 2000, 2001 and 2002, who were paid Livestock Premia and/or Arable Aid in one or more of those years and who continued to farm in 2005. The gross Single Payment is based on the average number of animals and/or the average number of hectares (in the case of Arable Aid) on which payments were made in the three reference years.

The new scheme will enable farmers to concentrate more on market requirements and will remove concerns about retention periods, quotas, stocking densities, census dates and other requirements associated with the old coupled schemes.

Payments under the 2005 Single Payment Scheme commenced on schedule on 1st December 2005 and over €1 billion was paid by December 31, 2005. Ireland was the only Member State to have commenced payments on December 1 and the only Member State to have made payments in full. The position at present is that some 126,000 farmers have been paid a total of €1,37 billion out of an estimated 128,000 that are due payments. Problems associated with Private Contract Clause (transfer of entitlements and inheritance cases) are the main issues holding up the remaining cases. Inheritance applications are still being received in the Department.

Under the Single Payment Scheme in its first year of operation, there were a number of additional measures that had to be processed. In summary these were:

- 17,500 applications under Force Majeure,

- 18,000 applications under new entrant/inheritance (applications under inheritance still being received),

- 6,000 applications to transfer entitlements under the so-called "Private Contract Clause".

- 12,500 applications to consolidate entitlements.

- 23,000 applications under the 2005 National Reserve (when account is taken of the number of farmers who applied under more than one category).

Cross-compliance

An important cornerstone of the decoupling of direct payments from production is the link between EU support for agriculture under the Single Payment Scheme and measures aimed at protecting the environment as well as achieving high standards in food safety and in animal health and welfare. Under the Single Payment Scheme farmers were required to respect the various Statutory Management Requirements (SMRs) set down in EU legislation (Directives and Regulations) on the environment, public animal and plant health and animal welfare and to maintain land in Good Agricultural and Environmental Condition (GAEC). This is known as Cross-Compliance.

Cross compliance therefore involves two key elements:

• A requirement for farmers to comply with 18 statutory management requirements (SMRs) set down in EU legislation on the **environment, food safety, animal health, welfare and plant health.**

And

• A requirement to maintain the farm in good agricultural and environmental condition (GAEC).

If an applicant is found to be non-compliant, sanctions are provided for in the governing EU regulations and those sanctions will be applied to the applicant's Single Payment.

Implementation of cross-compliance

The Cross compliance obligations are being phased in over a three-year period. Eight cross-compliance SMRs were introduced in 2005 together with the Good Agricultural and Environmental Condition requirements for Ireland.

A further seven SMRs have been introduced with effect from January 1, 2006 with the final three to be introduced with effect from January 1, 2007.

Before finalising the Guidance Document for 2005 cross compliance the Department sought views from interested stakeholders, in particular the farm bodies. The Department then published an information booklet for farmers in April 2005 covering the SMRs that were introduced in 2005. A copy of the booklet was posted to all farmers. The Department has since published a consultation document covering the SMRs to be introduced in 2006 and 2007 and this is available on the Department's website at www.agriculture.ie. The Department will now issue an information booklet to all farmers covering the new SMRs to be introduced in 2006 and 2007.

On-farm checks

In any given year, for the farmers selected for inspection, there will be two types of checks carried out for the purpose of implementing the Single Payment Scheme – Eligibility checks and Cross Compliance checks. The cross compliance checks are separate from eligibility checks (area checks).

Eligibility checks

In the first instance it is a requirement to carry out standard **eligibility** checks on 5% of farmers applying for the Single Payment Scheme. The requirements for checking eligibility of the area declared are similar to the arrangements in place over the years for area aid inspections. These checks will be carried out to:

• Verify that the actual area declared in the Single Payment Scheme application form corresponds with the area farmed by the applicant and to ensure there are no overlapping claims, or duplicate claims.

• Verify that the lands declared for set-aside purposes are maintained in accordance with the provisions of the EU Regulations and that the set-aside obligations are observed.

• Verify that the lands declared as permanent pasture have not, in fact, been ploughed and used for the growing of arable crops.

• Verify that the eligible hectares declared in the application form do not include land used for fruit or vegetables or potato production in the year of application.

• Verify that lands declared as eligible hectares have not been afforested or used for the production of other permanent crops in the year of application.

The level of cross compliance checking

The rate of on-farm inspection required for **cross-compliance** is 1% of those farmers to whom the Statutory Management Requirements or GAEC apply. However at least 5% of producers must be inspected under the Bovine Animal Identification and Registration requirements as this level is prescribed under the relevant Regulations.

Number of visits

In implementing the Single Payment Scheme, the policy of the Department is to minimise the number of inspection visits and to move towards a situation where, in most cases, all eligibility and cross-compliance checks will be carried out during a single farm visit.

The Department is committed to ensuring the maximum level of integration of inspections across all areas including inspections under the Disadvantaged Areas' Compensatory Allowance Scheme. This approach should minimise the level of inconvenience to farmers. This will also mean, for example, that control checks would be carried out in relation to eligibility of land declared, identification and registration of animals on the holding, and compliance with the various environmental Directives in one farm visit. However, in certain instances it will not be possible to avoid more than one visit to the same holding.

The sanctions level

During 2005, the Department engaged in protracted negotiations with the farming organisations in the context of a new Charter of Rights for farmers. During those negotiations a new system for delivering cross-compliance was agreed. The new system ensures that the rules will be applied in a uniform fashion throughout the country and that minor non-compliance that is not regarded as arising from negligence on behalf of the farmer will not lead to a financial penalty.

The National Reserve

Ireland's National Ceiling for 2005 is €1,260 million of which 3% (€37.8m) had been provisionally set aside to fund the National Reserve. The cost of funding successful applicants under Force Majeure and New Entrants during the reference period has meant that the sum of individual entitlements has exceeded our National ceiling requiring a 1.18% linear reduction of all entitlements. This linear reduction was accommodated within the 3% already deducted for the National Reserve. In effect therefore the ceiling overshoot amounts to some €15.1m while the sum of money available for the National Reserve amounts to €22.7m.

The National Reserve exists to try and minimise the impact on farmers who, for a variety of reasons, may find themselves disadvantaged in the transition to the new decoupled support regime as a result of changes in their businesses during or since the reference period. In particular the intention is to provide enhanced or new entitlements for certain farmers who made investments in production capacity or purchased or leased land on a long-term basis or who converted from dairying to a sector for which a direct payment would have been payable during the reference period. Such farmers, at the time when they took these decisions, had a legitimate expectation that the couple regime of direct payments would continue into the future.

There are four main categories under which farmers have applied for entitlements from the 2005 National Reserve: -

> **Category A:** Farmers who inherited or otherwise obtained a holding free of charge or for a nominal sum from a farmer who retired or died before May 16, 2005 where the holding was leased out

to a third party during the reference period.

Category B(i), B(ii), B(iii), and B(iv): Farmers who made an investment between January 1, 2000 and October 19, 2003, which resulted in an increase in production capacity. Investments can include purchase or long-term lease of land, purchase of suckler and/or ewe quota or other investments.

Category C: Farmers who sold their milk quota into a re-structuring scheme between January 1, 2000 and October 19, 2003 and who converted to a farming sector for which a direct payment under the Livestock and/or Arable Aid Schemes would have been payable in respect of the years 2000 to 2002.

Category D: New entrants to farming since December 31, 2002 and farmers who commenced farming in 2002 but who received no direct payments in that year. The applicant's total income may not exceed €40,000 and any off-farm income may not exceed €20,000. Farming qualifications are also required for this category and priority may be given to farmers under 35 years of age.

In addition, the cost of funding successful applicants under the following measures will have to be met from the pool of money in the National Reserve.

• Active dairy farmers who, because of force majeure, were unable to supply milk during the 2004/2005 milk quota year and were therefore allowed to temporarily lease out all or part of their quotas. The cost of awarding the equivalent of the decoupled dairy premium to these farmers must be met from the National Reserve.

• Sheep farmers with commonage land who, while farming very extensively, were prevented from expanding production during the period 1999 – 2002 pending the publication of commonage framework plans. (The number of applications received under this measure has been lower than expected with the result that the overall cost is likely to be in the region of €1m.)

There are mandatory and non-mandatory categories in the Reserve. In Ireland's case the mandatory categories are categories A, B(i), B(ii), B(iii), B(iv) and C. The non-mandatory categories are category D (new entrants) and certain hill sheep farmers who were prevented from increasing production during the reference period pending the publication of commonage framework plans. Separate application arrangements were in place for this latter group.

In allocating entitlements to successful applicants in the mandatory categories the Member State must apply objective criteria and ensure equal treatment between farmers. In the case of categories A and B(i) qualifying farmers will have declared hectares of land in 2005 that were free of entitlements and the intention to make an allocation in respect of those hectares based on objective criteria. It is envisaged that qualifying applicants under categories B(ii), B(iii), B(iv) and C will have their existing entitlements topped-up by a sum of money again determined on the basis of objective criteria.

In allocating entitlements to successful applicants in the non-mandatory categories the Member State must ensure that the allocation does not have the effect of increasing the value of any existing entitlements above the regional average value of entitlements. Similarly, the value of any new entitlements allocated to non-mandatory categories must not exceed the regional average. The Member State is allowed to determine what will constitute the regional average.

A Single Payment Advisory Committee was established comprising representatives of the farming organisations, Teagasc and officials from the Department to consider various aspects of the Reserve. These included the objective criteria that should be used in making allocations from the reserve to the mandatory categories and also the most appropriate way to determine what will constitute the regional average value of entitlements in the case of the non-mandatory categories.

The European Commission was also consulted in this regard and the Commission's legal advice was that, having established the regional average, the Member State is precluded from deviating from this figure by way of imposition of an overall cap mechanism or by way of application of a co-efficient. The Member State is also precluded from using a "hybrid" system, for example, the average of County and District Electoral Division (DED) averages. The Minister has decided that the regional average value of entitlements used in calculating National Reserve allocations in the appropriate categories would be the DED average.

The first tranche of allocations have already been made to successful applicants under the 2005 National Reserve. Some 5,000 successful applicants received National Reserve allocations worth €10.0 million.

Of the 17,500 farmers who applied to the 2005 National Reserve some 6,000 applied under more than one category. The regulations contain certain "anti-accumulation" clauses which mean that a farmer may not qualify for an allocation under two or more categories. In such circumstances an allocation will be made under the category that is most beneficial. About 3,800 applicants to the National Reserve have also applied under other measures, e.g. *force majeure* and new entrant during the reference period. The regulations provide that these farmers may not qualify under the reserve and under the other measures and because of this these 3,800 cases will have to be manually examined to see which measure is the most beneficial.

Modulation

Modulation is a process whereby each farmer's single payment is reduced by a set percentage (3% in 2005, rising to 4% in 2006 and 5% in 2007). Up to 80% of funds generated through modulation (about €34m in 2007) can be retained in Ireland for spending on certain Rural Development measures. The first tranche of funding will be available in 2006. The main Rural Development measures currently administered by this Department are the Disadvantages Areas' Compensatory Allowance Scheme, the Scheme for Early Retirement from Farming, the Rural Environment Protection Scheme and the Forestry Premium Scheme.

The new Council Regulation provides that new rural development measures may be introduced from 2006 in the areas of (a) food quality; (b) meeting standards, and (c) animal welfare. A consultative process took place within the Department on how modulated funds should be used in 2006. It was decided that the funds (some €18m) would be used to increase the level of payment under the Disadvantaged Areas Compensatory Allowance Scheme for 2006.

Trading of Single Payment entitlements for 2006

Application forms for the transfer and trading of entitlements in respect of the 2006 Single Payment Scheme are now available on the Department's website www.agriculture.ie The application form caters for the transfer of entitlements *with and without land* by way of sale, lease, gift or inheritance.

The sale of entitlements without land will only be permitted where at least 80% of the entitlements have been used in 2005, i.e. the farmer selling the entitlements must have declared enough land in 2005 to enable payment to be made on at least 80% of his/her entitlements.

Entitlements may only be leased/rented out if accompanied by the lease/rent of an equivalent number of eligible hectares.

Claw-back on sale of entitlements:

The levels of claw-back that will be applied to the selected transactions are as follows:

– Sales of entitlements without lands – 30%

– Sales of entitlements with lands where part of the holding is hold – 5%.

– Sales of entitlements with an entire holding – 2.5%.

No claw-back will apply in the following circumstances

– Where the effective date of the sale agreement was 21st December 2005 or earlier.

– Transfer of entitlements (with or without lands) by way of gift (within families) or inheritance.

– Lease of entitlements with land.

– Rental agreements in respect of entitlements with land.

– Sale of entitlements (with or without land) to new entrants to farming who satisfy certain criteria including age, income and educational qualifications.

– Sale of entitlements without land where the farmer selling used at least 80% of his entitlements in 2005, did not apply to consolidate, and is now simply selling the entitlements that were not used in 2005.

The Single Payment Scheme (SPS) application form

Each year, Single Payment Scheme (SPS) applicants will

receive an application form, and a Help Sheet which deals with the terms and eligibility conditions, and which should always be consulted and read carefully prior to completing the application form.

Based upon the limited experience to date, the Department of Agriculture and Food has identified a number of issues as being the most common cause of processing delays and/or reduced payments. It would therefore be imperative that applicants take careful note of these particular issues and avoid the identified pitfalls, so that they will receive their payment promptly and more importantly avoid the penalties which can be very significant, in that for example in 2006, a penalty of a 1% loss in payment for each working day that the application was received late, until a point was reached whereby a *total loss* of payment for applications received after the final cut-off point of May 18, 2006 was reached.

It is important to note that one entitlement is equal to one eligible hectare of land, therefore if you have 20 entitlements you must declare 20 eligible hectares in order to benefit from the full Single Payment. Applicants must ensure that they do not over claim on the area of a parcel of land, so care must be taken to make appropriate deductions where necessary for buildings, farm yards, woods and dense scrubland for example.

Each land parcel is allocated its own unique land parcel number (LPIS), which is in effect a reference area, and where an applicant claims a greater area, with respect to the particular land parcel number, this could give rise to an over claim, and possibly a penalty.

In order to avoid this problem arising, if an applicant is adding any new parcel of land to his or her holding in any year, he or she must obtain the land parcel number from the previous occupier, and enter the number in the appropriate column on the application form.

If there is no land parcel number available, applicants should identify the new plot or plots in the appropriate column by designating them as Plot 1, Plot 2 or Plot 3 as required, and clearly identify such plots on an Ordnance Survey map or Land Registry map, and these must accordingly be submitted with the application.

It is essential when making the application to declare all the parcels of land in your holding, as there is a penalty imposed where a parcel is subsequently discovered (probably in the course of an eligibility check) that should have been on the application form. Likewise, all supporting documentation such as maps, evidence of commonage should be submitted with the SPS application as appropriate. Where necessary, an applicant should enter or amend, the ten month start date for each land parcel or plot declared on the application form.

Applicants should pay particular attention to the closing date for SAS applications, as the penalties for late applications are quite severe. It therefore goes without saying that within one week of the day of receipt of the SPS application form, the applicant should complete same (takes less than fifteen minutes) and send it to the Single Payment Scheme Unit in the pre-addressed envelope provided by the Department of Agriculture and Food.

It is the author's experience that in the past problems have often arisen for applicants due to not being in a position to furnish proof of posting prior to the closing date. In fairness, the Department of Agriculture and Food has attempted to address this difficulty by attaching to the envelope provided, a certificate of posting which records the fee paid for posting, the officer's signature, the address, the stamped date of posting, and the acceptance reference number, all of which in effect constitutes the applicant's receipt of posting, and which would form essential evidence for the applicant should the application form become lost or mislaid or fails to reach the addressee either in time or at all.

CHAPTER 4

Planning Law

Planning law and the farmer

The farmer like every other citizen, is subject to a legislative code which governs any development which they wish to carry out upon their farm, and ever since the Planning and Development Act 1963, which came into operation on October 1, 1964, the first thing that a farmer has to do is to consider whether any development which he undertakes falls within the concept of development as defined by section 3 of the Planning and Development Act 1963, or is exempted development. Therefore it is extremely important to ascertain what development is, because planning permission is prima facia required for all development and planning control is exercised against unauthorised developments.

It is clear, that the Planning and Development Act 2002, which incorporates significant elements of the 1963 Act and it is clear from section 2 of the Planning and Development Act 2000, that planning permission is required in respect of all developments of land other than exempted development and in respect of retention of unauthorised development.

Development as defined in section 3 of the Act is carrying out of any work on, in, over or under land or the making of any material change in the use of any structures on the land. Land for the purpose of the Act includes any structure and any land covered with water. Therefore it is clear that development encompasses two issues:

  (a) the carrying out of works, and
  (b) any material change of use.

It is therefore important to determine into which category a particular development falls in order to determine what provisions of the Acts or Regulations applies.

Works are broadly defined in section 1 as including any act or operation of construction, excavation, demolition, extension, alteration, repair or renewal and in relation to a protected structure or proposed protected structure, includes any act or operation involving the application or removal of plaster, paint, wallpaper, tiles or other material to or from the surfaces of the interior or exterior of a structure.

Planning law from the perspective of the farmer, therefore is significant from the point of view of an application, in so far as there is significant procedural issues that must be strictly complied with, and there is literally no room for manoeuvre as the Planning Authorities are statutorily bound to ensure that each procedure is followed when they commence to process an application.

Section 3 of the Local Government (Planning and Development) Act 1963, defined the concept of development. It stated as follows:-

> "Save where the context requires otherwise the carrying out of works on, in or under land, or the making of any material change in the use of any structure or other land".

For the purpose of the Planning Acts and Regulations, development is divided into two broad categories:

- The carrying out of works on, in or under land (works in this context is defined as including any act or operation of construction, excavation, demolition, extension, alteration, repair or renewal).

- The making of any material change in the use of any structures or other land. In this regard land "includes any structure, and structure includes the land on which the structure is situated where the context so admits". This second category includes such changes emanated from the act of building, demolition, extension, alteration, repair or renewal.[1]

Therefore it is important to understand what development is from the perspective of the process of seeking planning permission, and where unauthorised developments take place, Local Authorities are empowered to take enforcement action.

Section 4(1) of the Planning and Development Act 2000, exempts a significant number of Local Authority developments that can be carried out by the Local Authority.

Therefore, the area of planning and development has been significantly revolutionised by the introduction of the Planning and Development Act 2000, and the Planning and Development Regulations 2001[2] and the Planning and Development Regulations 2002,[3] and these have been in operation since March 11, 2002. The introduction of this new legislative code has reduced and to an extent streamlined this area of law.

The primary focus of our chapter will be in relation to planning and development requirements that are imposed upon the farming environment, but nevertheless it is important to note that the planning code is a self contained statutory code, and that a failure to comply with the statutory requirements as laid down in the said code could well result in a decision of the Planning Authority being quashed for invalidity.

Indeed in an important decision and which emphasised the need to strictly comply with the requirements laid down

---

[1] See O'Sullivan and Shepard, *Irish Planning Law in Practice,* (Butterworths, Dublin).
[2] S.I. No. 600 of 2001.
[3] S.I. No. 70 of 2002.

in the planning code, Henchy J. in *Monaghan UDC v. Alphabet Promotions Limited* stated:

> "What the legislature has prescribed or allowed to be prescribed in such circumstances as necessary should be treated by the Courts as nothing short of necessary and any deviation from the requirements must, before it can be overlooked, be shown, by the person seeking to have it excused, to be so trivial, or so technical, or so peripheral, or otherwise so insubstantial that, on the principle that it is the spirit rather than the letter of the law that matters, the prescribed obligations has been substantially and therefore adequately complied with."[4]

The strictures laid down by Mr. Justice Henchy in the foregoing decision, found even greater emphasis in the Planning and Development Regulations, which followed the implementation of the Planning and Development Act 2000.

The Regulations set out in great detail, the importance of the public being made aware of the fact that an application for planning permission is being made, and within a period of two weeks prior to the making of a planning application, and lodging same with the Planning Authority, an applicant for planning permission must place a notice in a newspaper (either a national or local) which is circulating in the area, and also must erect a site notice in a place that is readily visible to the public.

It is the author's experience, that Planning Authorities are paying particular attention to contents of the newspaper notice, and in particular are ensuring strict adherence to the legal requirements as to the content of the newspaper notice

---

[4]   [1980] I.L.R.M. 64.

as set out in article 18 of the 2001 Planning and Development Regulations.

Members of the general public are entitled to be in a position, when they peruse the newspaper notice, to know the name of the applicant, the exact townland and location of the land to which the application relates and the nature of the permission being sought, as to whether it is for ordinary planning permission, outline planning permission or indeed permission consequent to the grant of outline planning permission, and the exact nature and extent of the development.

There is also the additional requirement to state at the end of the newspaper notice, that the planning application may be inspected or purchased at the office of the Planning Authority and a submission or observation in relation to the application may be made to the Planning Authority in writing on payment of the prescribed fee within the period of five weeks beginning on the date of receipt by the authority of the application.

Likewise, article 19 of the Regulations specifies the exact requirements that the site notice must contain. It must be inscribed or printed in indelible ink on a white background and affixed on a rigid or durable material and secured against damage from bad weather or other causes. Therefore when one is erecting the site notice, it should be erected on a solid material, such as a pole specially put in place for the purpose, and if the application pertains to a development, which is some way in off the road, the site notice must nevertheless be erected in a position that is clearly visible from the public road, and where members of the public can read the contents thereof.

Article 20 of the Regulations provides that the site notice shall be maintained in position on the land or structure concerned for a period of five weeks from the date of furnishing the planning application to the Planning Authority and if it falls or is removed in some fashion, it must be replaced or renewed.

Indeed very often, if the local area engineer, who will visit the site for the purpose of dealing with issues pertaining to site distance and percolation issues for example, happens to visit the site on the last day of the five week period, from the date of receipt of the planning application, and the particular site notice was missing or had fallen or was not in a visible position, the planning application would be retuned to the applicant and he or she will have to commence the process again. This will entail having to resubmit the newspaper notice and re-erect the site notice, and apart altogether from the additional financial outlay that will be incurred, there will also be a further five-week time lag at least.

Again it is imperative that the site notice is signed by the applicant, or his duly appointed agent, and it must contain the signature and address of such agent who is acting on behalf of the applicant and must state clearly the date upon which the site notice was erected.

Article 22 of the said Regulations set out the contents of the planning application, together with the documents, which must accompany the application. Such documents include copies of the plans, which must include a site or layout plan and drawings of the floor plans, elevations and sections, and must comprehensively describe the works to which the application relates. Again a copy of the site notice must also be submitted, and the location of the site notice must be marked on the site location map. The appropriate planning fee must also accompany the planning application, and which must be lodged within two weeks of the newspaper notice being placed in the newspaper circulating in the locality.

It goes without saying, that a full copy of the newspaper, which contains the newspaper notice, which should be for convenience outlined in red ink on the said newspaper, should also accompany the planning application.

Upon receipt of the planning application, the planning

authority must stamp each document with the date of receipt of same. It will also consider whether the applicant has complied with the requirements in relation to the newspaper notice, the site notice and examine as to whether the necessary documents are accompanying the application.

The Planning Authority will also pay particular attention as to whether the address or location of the area to which the planning application refers, has been adequately set out, and particular care is taken so as to ensure that the public are not misled in any way as to the precise location, which relates to the particular application.

Article 26 states that where a Planning Authority consider the documents as submitted, and is satisfied that it has complied with the various articles pertaining to the site notice, newspaper notice and nature and extent of the plans submitted, they will then send an acknowledgement to the applicant, stating the date of receipt of the application.

If the Planning Authority is of the opinion, that any or all of the requirements of the Articles hereinabove referred to have not been complied with, or for any reason, they will deem the planning application invalid. They will specify the particular Regulation that the applicant has failed to comply with and the Planning Authority is obliged to return to the applicant the planning application and all the documents that accompanied same and contemporaneously enters details of the invalid application in the planning register. Of course the planning fee must also be returned, and if somebody has made an observation or submission in relation to the application, in the interim, such persons or bodies must also be notified that the application for permission by the applicant has been deemed invalid.

Article 27 provides that a Planning Authority must also make available a list of planning applications received by the Planning Authority during the previous week, and it is noted that Planning Authorities now are submitting same to newspapers circulating in the locality, and again giving the public an opportunity to read in their local newspaper, which generally circulates on a weekly basis, the fact that an application has been made for a particular development in a particular area a week or so previously.

If somebody who wished to make a submission or observation thereon, has missed the original notice of application, then they have a further opportunity of being alerted by this process and of course they would then have an opportunity to make the observation or submission within the statutory period of five weeks prescribed therefor by article 29 of the said Regulations.

Notice to certain bodies

Article 28 of the Planning and Development Regulations, 2001, sets out in detail a number of bodies to which a Planning Authority must give notice of a planning application, which has been validly received by the Local Authority. The prescribed bodies include:-

• An Taisce.

• Department of Environment and Local Government.

• The National Roads Authority.

• The Heritage Council.

• The relevant Regional Fisheries Boards.

• The Minister for the Marine and Natural Resources.

• Bord Fáilte Éireann.

• An Chomairle Ealáion.

• Waterways Ireland.

When the Local Authority is notifying the prescribed bodies, they must send them a copy of the planning application and indicate the date of receipt of the application and also specify that any submissions or observations must be made within five weeks of the date of receipt and if they are so received that they would be taken into consideration by the Planning Authority when reaching its decision on the application. Once the Local Authority receives a written submission or observation from such bodies, they must be duly acknowledged by the Planning Authority in writing.

Article 29 is an enabling provision, which permits any person or body who pays the prescribed fee, which is currently €20, can make a submission or observation in writing to the Planning Authority in relation to the planning application and again this must be done within a period of five weeks beginning on the date of receipt by the Local Authority of the application. Again the Planning Authority must acknowledge receipt of the submission or observation in writing.

It is noted that where a submission or observation is received outside of the five week time period, the Planning Authority cannot consider same and it must return the submission or observation together with the fee and notify the person or body, that their observation or submission cannot be considered because it is outside the statutory time period provided therefor.

It is the general practice of a Planning Authority that they will not take any steps in relation to a planning application that they receive, until the five-week period has elapsed. Obviously this is to facilitate people making submissions or observations in relation to the application itself.

In any event, the Planning Authority must deal with the planning application within eight weeks of the receipt of the application and a failure to do so within that requisite period, will lead to a default permission, whereby it is deemed, the decision by the Planning Authority to grant permission is regarded as having been given on the last day of the period of eight weeks. This is something that would rarely happen nowadays, but nevertheless adherence to strict statutory time limits must be strictly complied with and a failure by either the applicant or the Planning Authority to adhere to the stipulated time periods, as laid down in the regulations, have significant repercussions for either party involved.

Article 33 of the Planning and Development Regulations, 2001, enables the Planning Authority, where it has received a valid planning application where same has been considered, to within eight weeks of the said application require the applicant to submit further information.

Once a notice seeking such additional or further information is furnished by the Planning Authority, the applicant has six months to comply with the request for further information, and if the applicant fails to do so, within the time limit of six months, the application shall be deemed to be withdrawn.

Once an applicant responds to the request for further information, the Planning Authority must determine the application within four weeks of the receipt of the additional information. The only exception to this may arise where the Planning Authority within the four week period might have to resort to seeking verification of some matter which might be ambiguous and not fully set out, or which might lead to misunderstanding.

Sometimes, further information might contain significant new material, or contain revised plans or drawings, which in the opinion of the Planning Authority amounts to significant new information. In that event, article 35 of the 2001 Planning and Development Regulations, requires the Planning Authority to notify the prescribed bodies under article 28, as referred to hereinabove, together with any other person who has made a valid observation or submission in relation to the planning application.

This therefore allows the prescribed bodies or other persons, who do not fall into that category, and who have made initial observations or submissions, to make further submissions or observations, in relation to the significant new information that has been furnished by the applicant. Likewise the Planning Authority must request the applicant to publish in the newspaper circulating in the locality the further notice, which informs the public that significant additional and new information has been submitted in relation to his or her planning application.

Time limits

Section 34(8) of the Planning and Development Act 2000, specifies the time periods within which the Planning Authority must determine a planning application.

As stated hereinabove, where a Planning Authority fails to make a decision within the requisite period, a default permission arises by virtue of the fact that the decision of the Planning Authority is deemed to have been made granting such planning permission on the last day of the specified period, which is eight weeks from the date of receipt of the application.

Once within that eight-week period, the Planning Authority has sought further and additional information, same must be replied to within six months, but in any event the Planning Authority must determine the application within four weeks of the receipt of the additional information. It should also be noted, that pursuant to section 34(9) of the Planning and Development Act 2000, it is provided, that the applicant may consent in writing to the extension of the period of time for determining the application.

It should also be noted, this is of particular interest to the agricultural community, that where an application is made to erect a dwelling house on lands, which abut or are adjacent to a national primary route, that notice of such an application must be furnished to the National Road Authority, and they are entitled to make submissions in relation to such an application to the Planning Authority from the perspective of safety and any other concerns they might have in relation to traffic hazards generated by such traffic movements that would emerge on to the national primary route from any gateway or opening that would lead on to the said public highway.

The Planning Authority having made a decision to grant or refuse a person the application as sought must within three working days of the decision being made notify the applicant of the decision and likewise any person or bodies, both prescribed and otherwise, who made submissions or observations in respect thereof. Again, it is noted that when one peruses the weekly newspapers in provincial areas, that the list of decisions made on planning applications in the previous week are printed, and again this is something that is provided for in article 32 of the Planning and Development Regulations 2001.

Appeals

If a person feels aggrieved by a decision of the Planning Authority, he or she can appeal against the decision to grant planning permission subject to or without conditions, or to refuse same. This appeals procedure is now set out in section 37 of the Planning and Development Act 2000, and Part VII of the Planning and Development Regulations 2001. Indeed it should be noted that under section 139 of the Planning and Development Act 2000, an appeal can be made only in relation to a condition or conditions, which the grant of planning permission has been subject to.

It is obviously clear that the applicant for permission who feels aggrieved by a decision of the Planning Authority can appeal against a decision particularly whereby if a Planning Authority refused to grant him or her the permission sought. Again one would anticipate that the persons or bodies who made submissions or observations in writing in relation to the application for planning permission, or likewise are in a position to appeal against the decision if they feel so aggrieved by it.

Section 37(6)(a) of the Planning and Development Act 2000, also enables a person who has an interest in land adjoining land in respect of which the planning permission has been granted, to apply to the Board for leave to appeal against the particular decision, and in so doing they must outline in writing the name and address of the person making application, the grounds upon which the application is made and a description of the person's interest in the adjacent land.

In general, the circumstances in which leave will be granted, where the applicant shows:

• That the development for which the planning permission has been granted differs materially from the development as set out in the application for permission, by reason of conditions imposed by the Planning Authority, and,

• That the imposition of such conditions will materially affect the applicant's enjoyment of his land or will reduce the value thereof.

Nevertheless, the Planning and Development Act 2000, has greatly restricted the number of persons who can make an appeal against a decision now to An Bord Pleanála, because under the 1963 Act any person had a right of appeal to An Bord Pleanála irrespective of whether they took part in the original planning process or had any material interest in the adjacent lands. From the perspective of the agricultural community, this is a welcome development as it circumscribes the numbers of people who can appeal to An Bord Pleanála in relation to a decision and diminishes the opportunity for frivolous or vexatious appeals.

Appeals to An Bord Pleanála are again subject to strict time limits, and the appeal must be initiated within four weeks beginning on the day of the decision of the Planning Authority. Obviously the appeal must be made in writing stating clearly the name and address of the appellant and the subject matter of the appeal. Again, it is necessary to set out in full the grounds of appeal and the reasons, considerations and arguments on which they are based.

Further for an appeal to be valid, it must be accompanied by the prescribed fee and if an appeal has been made by a person or body who made submissions or observations in relation to the original planning application, it must be accompanied by the relevant acknowledgement, which he or she or they have received from the Planning Authority, upon receipt of their relevant submissions or observations.

Any person making an appeal to An Bord Pleanála must ensure that the grounds of appeal are comprehensive in nature, and if one is making an appeal, one should adopt the "one bite of the cherry" principle in relation to submission prepared concerning the grounds of appeal or referral. An Bord Pleanála has full original jurisdiction, in so far it is entitled to request any party to appeal or person(s) or body making submissions or observations to the Bord, to make further submissions or observations in relation to any matter that might have arisen and will request them to submit further documents or particulars or other information that the Bord regards important for the proper disposal of appeals.

Of course, if a particular party either, the applicant or indeed the person(s) making observations or submissions, respond to such request from An Bord Pleanála, by submitting significant particulars or other information, in the context of the requirements of natural and constitutional justice, the other party who has not made such a submission, is entitled to at least copies of this additional information and to make a comprehensive response thereto.

Upon receipt of the appeal by An Bord Pleanála, the Bord sends a copy of the appeal to both the Planning Authority and the Appellant. Each then have four weeks to make submissions and observations in writing to the Bord in relation to the appeal or referral. Likewise any person other than a party to an appeal may also make submissions or observations in writing but again this must be done within four weeks of the date of receipt of the appeal by An Bord Pleanála.

Further, once an appeal is made to An Bord Pleanála, the relevant Planning Authority has two weeks, beginning on the day on which a copy of the appeal is sent to it by the Bord, in which to submit certain documents to the Bord. It is also required to make a copy of the appeal available for inspection during office hours at the office of the Local Authority until the matter is disposed of and to notify relevant parties of the fact of the appeal.

It should also be noted, that An Bord Pleanála may in its absolute discretion hold an oral hearing into the matter. Again the request for an oral hearing by any party to an appeal should be made in writing to the Bord and should be accompanied by the relevant fee. Parties to the hearing must be given not less than a week's notice to the hearing unless a further period is agreed. The Bord has an absolute discretion to dismiss an appeal where it considers that it is frivolous or vexatious, or without substance or foundation or made with the sole intention of delaying the development without substance or further information.

As stated hereinbefore, the Bord has full original jurisdiction, and can overturn the decision of the Planning Authority.

The Bord is also required to have regard to any guidelines issues by the Minister for the Environment and Local Government to Planning Authorities and to government and ministerial policies.

Section 126(1) of the Planning and Development Act 2000, specifies that it is the duty of the Planning Bord to ensure that as far as practicable that appeals and referrals are disposed of as expeditiously as possible. The stated period within which the Bord must make its decision is eighteen weeks, although if this is not possible, or appropriate giving the nature of a particular appeal, or that the Bord has a particular large number of appeals on hand, the Bord is entitled to extend the period within which to make its decision, but it must inform all the relevant parties of this fact.

Once the Bord makes an appeal in relation to any matter that has been referred to it, it is obliged to inform all relevant parties of the decision.

Planning and development requirements that are imposed upon a farm_environment

It is important to analyse the impact of the legislative code upon farming and as to what exactly constitutes exempted development in an agricultural environment and further we will examine what constitutes rural development within the definitions provided in the regulatory framework.

Definition of Agriculture

Section 2 of the Planning and Development Act 2000, agriculture is defined widely and includes:

- horticulture,

- fruit growing, seed growing,

- dairy farming,

- the breeding and keeping of livestock (including any creature kept for the production of food, wool, skins or fur or for the purpose of its use in farming land),

- the training of horses and the rearing of bloodstock,

- the use of land as grazing land, meadow land, osier land, market garden, nursery ground

and it is stipulated that agriculture shall be construed accordingly.

There are two fundamental differences in this definition

from that which prevailed under the previous planning acts.

The first point to note is that turbary which is effectively bog land and forestry are excluded from the definitional remit and its absence speaks volumes for recent legislative interventions. The second point is that the definition now specifically includes the training of horses and the rearing of livestock which as we will subsequently see, places both of those categories of activity within the context of exempted development under the statute. It is clear from the definition provided under the legislation that most categories of farming and/or agricultural endeavour are now encompassed within the legislative code.

Section 32 of the Planning and Development Act 2002, provides that planning permission is required for any development of land which is not "exempted development" as defined under the Act. Further and to that end we shall examined what exactly is exempted from the requirements to apply for planning permission for development.

Exempted development

Section 4 of the 2000 Act provides a list of the specific categories of development which will constitute exempted development.

The Planning and Development Regulations set out at Schedule II, Part III thereof, and the exemptions that apply in the context of rural development which we will look at presently.

Section 4(a) of the Planning and Development Act provides that the following are to be *exempted developments:*

> (a) development consisting of the use of any land for the purpose of agriculture and development consisting of the use for that purpose of any building occupied together with land so used.

This is effectively regarded as the agricultural exemption, which consists of the use of lands or buildings on that land. It is to be noted at this juncture the definition contained in section 2 only extends to "the use" of land and not to any material works required to establish the land into a position where such use is tenable.

What is development?

At this point it might be useful to actually define what development is within the Act. Section 3(1) of the Planning and Development Act 2000, provides that development means, except where the context otherwise requires the carrying out of any work on, in, over or under land or the making of any material change in the use of any structures or other land. It has to be noted at this point that development, use and works all have a different statutory definition (see above).

The Planning and Development Regulations 2001, at Schedule II, Part III thereof, define and deal with the exemption in the context of exempted rural development.

It should be noted that these are not absolute exemptions and that they can be the subject of restrictions when and where appropriate (for example see article 9 of the Planning and Development Regulations 2001). That proviso aside, there are in effect seventeen categories of exempted developments which have brought about many changes which in themselves have led to a restriction and reduction on the size of exempted developments permitted on agricultural land.

Summarily, Classes 3, 4, 5, 6 through 10, 11 deal with the substantive issues to which attention will be drawn at this juncture. That is not to say that more specialised areas as contained in the other categories will not be of interest to many readers. The Planning and Development Regulations 2001, should be referred to where more specialised categories of exceptions are outlined in full and is available on the

Government website under the Irish Statute Book.

Classes 3 and 4

This exemption deals with minor works and structures. Such work extend to the construction and maintenance of ponds, drains, gullies, the widening of watercourses and the creation of facilities such as embankments in order to provide for same are exempted.

Category 4 provides that the erection of fencing below two metres within the area of a house is exempted.

Other exemptions

Classes 6, 7, 8, 9 & 10

The exemptions contained between categories 6 and 10 inclusive of the Planning and Development Regulations 2001, are those of the greatest concern to the majority of industrial farmers as, in summary, they deal with the provision of structures for the storage of animals and general storage areas including silage pits, yards, milking parlours, stores, barns, sheds, glass houses, training structures to name but a few.

Class 6 of Schedule II, Part III, deals specifically with the provision of rural *structures for the housing of animals*. Class 6 provides that the works are to consist of a roof structure, a floor area of which does not exceed two hundred square metres. It is to be used for the housing of deer, horses, donkeys, cattle, sheep or goats.

Restrictions on exemptions

There are however as already alluded to, strict limitations placed upon this exemption.

The first of those major restrictions is that the entire floor space of such structure or any other such structure situated within the same farm yard complex and/or within one hundred metres of that complex shall *not* exceed three hundred square metres gross floor space when added together.

The second major restriction is that no such structure which is within one hundred metres of a public road shall exceed eight metres in height. Thirdly, in relation to effluent storage facilities, each and all effluent storage facilities although not counted in terms of square footage contribution to the overall aggregate square footage of the development, must be constructed in strict compliance of the Department of Agriculture and Food, and Department of Environment requirements and must seriously take into consideration all concerns in relation to water quality and/or water pollution.

Category 7 exemptions deal with somewhat smaller housing operations for somewhat smaller animals. The provisions run parallel to those of class 6 and extend to mink, poultry and pigs. The development however may not exceed seventy-five square metres. And the requirements placed upon those developments which would fall into class six are reflected here also.

- The gross floor space of any area of such a structure coupled with any other structure situated in the same complex or farmyard shall not exceed one hundred square metres in aggregate.

- No structure shall be situated nor shall any effluent be stored within one hundred metres of any house nor within ten metres of any public road.

- The same requirement apply in relation to effluent storage as they do to category 6, and finally and applicable to both categories 6 and 7, the building must be used for agricultural uses.

The third major category of exemption within Schedule II, Part III, is the class 8 exemption which extends to *roofless cubicles, yards, silage storage areas, silos, assembly yards, milking parlours or silage production facilities* having a similar character or description which has in excess of two hundred square metres floor space with but not including ancillary effluent storage provision. Again the point has to be made here that the six requirements listed previously in relation to categories 6 and 7 apply equally here to class 8.

The class 9 exemptions are contained in the Planning and Development Regulations 2001, Schedule II, Part III, is basically a catch all provision which is to cover any building which has not already been specified within classes 6, 7 or 8 and which has a gross floor space not exceeding three hundred square metres. Included under this heading are glasshouses, sheds, storage areas and barns.

There are some subtle distinctions within this category in relation to the restrictions that are to be placed upon the usage of these structures:

- The gross floor space of any such structure other than such structures situated within the same farm complex or farmyard shall not exceed nine hundred square metres gross floor space.

- The structures are to be used for purposes solely in conjunction with agriculture or forestry and not for the housing of animals or the storing of effluent.

- No such structure shall be located within a hundred metres of any house or residential building, school, hospital, church or building used for public assembly without the written consent of the owner or occupier. Also same structure may not be situated within ten metres of any public road.

- No structure shall exceed eight metres in height when within one hundred metres of any public road.

- A restriction which applies to each category 6, 7, 8 and 9, is that no unpainted metal sheeting shall be used for the roofing or the external finish of the structure.

Class 10 provides for the exempted development of any *open-air structure in a rural area which provides for the training or exercising of horses* or ponies together with a drainage bed or all weather surface. The requirements are as follows:

- The structure must be used for the training of horses or the exercising of horses.

- These areas and these structures will not be used for public events.

- The structures shall not exceed two metres in height, and finally,

- The structure must not be situated within ten metres of any public road.

Finally, in relation to class 11 which is extrinsically linked to classes to 3 and 4, the Planning and Development Regulations provide for land reclamation in rural areas. The following works are exempt if carried out on land used for agriculture or forestry purposes *only.*

- Field drainage,

- Land reclamation,

- The removal of fences,

- The improvement of existing fences,

- The improvement of hill grazing, and

- The reclamation of estuarine marsh land or of callows where the preservation of such land or callows is not an objective of a development plan for the area.

It is noteworthy that this category at class 11 is effectively a replication of the exemption which was provided in the previous legislative code under the 1963 Planning and Development legislation. The decision of the High Court in

Irish Wild Bird Conservancy and Clonakilty Golf and Country Club Limited,[5] is a very persuasive, if not binding, authority in this situation, which would lend itself to the argument that exempted development extends only to the use and not to the carrying out of works for such purposes. Costello J. in that case held that because the works on the land constituted a material change in use, they could no longer fall within the exempted development category and as a result constituted unauthorised development for which planning permission was in fact required.

A warning should be sounded at this point, that although the above listed categories of development are exempted from the requirements to obtain planning permission, the restrictions placed on those exemptions are quite strict. If development of existing structures upon the land will take persons outside of these exemptions, then it is at the very least strongly advised that planning permission is sought for such developments, as the consequences of unauthorised development and the enforcement of planning requirements have onerous consequences.

Forestry

In relation to the development of forestry, it was recognised at the outset that forestry has been removed from the statutory definition of agriculture. It should be noted, however, that section 4 of the Planning and Development Act 2000, provides for the thinning, felling and replanting of trees, forest and woodland, and also the construction and maintenance and improvement of non-public roads in order to service such woodlands.

The prior code that existed under the 1963 legislation left the planning of forestry exempt from planning permission requirements, however, the changes that have been introduced

---

[5]   Unreported High Court, Costello J., July 23, 1996,

by the 2000 Act mean that the planting of initial forestry and turbary are no longer exempt under the general agricultural exemptions. There are specific exemptions in relation to limited and localised replacement of forestry contained in the subsequent Regulations.[6]

---

[6]   For a detailed examination of the entitlements, see Class 16 and Class 15 of Sch.II, Pt III of the Planning and Development Regulations 2001.

CHAPTER 5

Farming and the Environment

The Nitrates Directive

Introduction

The Nitrates Directive was introduced in 1991.[1] Its core objective is the protection of waters against pollution and in particular eutrophication, and the prevention of new sources of water pollution. The term "eutrophication" refers to a process whereby water becomes enriched with plant nutrients, such as phosphorus and nitrogen leading to a reduction in dissolved oxygen in the water. Eutrophication of a water body results in a significantly reduced capacity of the water body to support aquatic life. A particular objective of the Nitrates Directive is to control water pollution caused by the increased use of artificial fertilisers containing nitrates in agriculture.

The Directive obliges each EU Member State to designate nitrate vulnerable zones in accordance with certain fixed criteria. The decisive criterion is whether the nitrate content of the water exceeds or risked exceeding 50mg per litre or whether the waters were eutrophic.

In zones designated "nitrate vulnerable," Member States were required to establish national action programmes which must contain measures prohibiting the use of certain fertilisers during certain periods and restricting the amount of livestock manure applied to the land per year to not more than 170kg

---

[1] Directive 91/679—Concerning the protection of waters against pollution caused by nitrates from agriculture.)

of nitrogen. Implementation of the Nitrates directive throughout the EU has been poor, and by the end of 2004, only Denmark, France and Luxembourg had implemented the Directive.

Implementation of Nitrates Directive in Ireland

The implementation of the Nitrates Directive in Ireland has proved particularly difficult. The Nitrates Directive has been implemented through a number of statutes and regulations. The European Communities (Protection of Waters against Pollution from Agricultural Sources) Regulations 2003 designated all of Ireland for the purposes of protecting water quality against nitrate pollution from agricultural sources.

However, Ireland failed to establish and implement a national action programme to the satisfaction of the EU Commission. In a decision in 2004 the European Court of Justice held that Ireland had failed to establish and implement an action programme required by the Nitrates Directive. For this reason Ireland was obliged to introduce new measures to satisfy the EU Commission that it had properly implemented the Nitrates directive.

After prolonged negotiations agreement was finally reached with the EU Commission on a national action programme. As a result of this agreement, on December 12, 2005 the Regulations formally implementing the Directive into Irish Law, the European Communities (Good Agricultural Practice for the Protection of Waters) Regulations 2005,[2] were signed into law. As we will see below they had a short shelf life as the farming community mobilised significant opposition to certain aspects of same, which culminated in significant amendments being made thereto, and the consequent revocation of S.I. 788 of 2005, and its replacement with S.I. No. 378 of 2006.

---

[2]   S.I. No. 788 of 2005.

The Nitrates Regulations

Introduction

The European Communities (Good Agricultural Practice for Protection of Waters) Regulations ("the Regulations") gave effect to Ireland's National Action Programme agreed with the EU in December 2005. The Regulations are complex and highly technical in nature. They may be conveniently be considered under the following headings:

- General Obligations.

- Farmyard Management.

- Minimisation of soiled water.

- Capacity of storage facilities.

- Exemptions to the storage capacity requirements.

- Nutrient Management.

- Prevention of water pollution from fertilisers and certain activities.

- The organic nitrogen limit.

- The relationship between the Regulations and REPS.

- The administration and enforcement of the Regulations.

- Offences under the Regulations.

General obligations

They impose two general obligations on all occupiers of agricultural holdings. The first general obligation is to ensure compliance with the provisions of the Regulations in relation to that holding. The second general obligation is to have regard to any advice or guidelines which may be issued by the Department of Agriculture and Food or the EPA. At the date of writing such guidelines have not yet been issued.

However the Department of Agriculture and Food has indicated it is preparing a detailed explanatory handbook and guidelines on the operation of the Regulations.

Farmyard management

Part 2 of the Regulations contains detailed and technical provisions regulating all aspects of farmyard management. The underlying objective of these provisions is to prevent water pollution. In practical terms the obligations imposed by the Regulations is adopt the "best practice" in farmyard management. Thus, the obligations imposed by the Regulations in respect of the application of fertiliser substantially mirror the technical advice furnished by TEAGASC.

In this regard the regulations will not impose any great burden on farmers who are already applying farmyard management practices in accordance with TEAGASC advice and general good practice. Such farmers will already (or with minor changes) be in a position to be compliant with the requirements of the nitrates Regulations in relation to farmyard management.

Minimisation of soiled water

Article 4 of the Regulations impose a general obligation on an occupier of an agricultural holding to take "all such reasonable steps as are necessary" for the purposes of minimising the amount of soiled water produced on the holding. In addition there is an obligation to ensure that "all reasonable steps as are necessary" are taken to ensure that rainwater from roofs and unsoiled paved areas and water flowing from higher ground onto a farmyard is diverted to a clean water outfall, and prevented from entering onto soiled paved areas or otherwise becoming soiled.

The term "soiled water" is defined for the purposes of

Article 4 of the Regulations as water arising from concreted areas, hard standings areas, holding areas for livestock and other farmyard areas where such water is contaminated by contact with livestock faeces or urine or silage effluent, chemical fertilisers, washings such as vegetable washings, milking parlour washings or washings from mushrooms houses, and water used in washing farm equipment. Specifically excluded from the definition of soiled water is any liquid which has either:

(a) A biochemical oxygen demand exceeding 2,500 mg per litre; or
(b) a dry matter content exceeding 1%.[3]

However, the provisions of Article 4 do not come into operation until January 1, 2007.

Article 5 of the Regulations requires that livestock and other organic fertilisers, soiled water and effluents from dungsteads, farmyard manure pits, and silage pits arising or produced in a building or a yard on a holding shall prior to its application to land or other treatment be collected and held in a manner that prevents the run-off seepage, directly or indirectly, into groundwater or surface waters of such substances.

Article 6 of the Regulations requires that such storage facilities be maintained free of structural defect. In addition such storage facilities must be "designed, sited, constructed, maintained and managed so as to prevent run-off or seepage, directly or indirectly, into groundwater or surface water". As and from August 1, 2006, any such storage facilities must also be constructed in accordance with Department of Food and Agriculture specifications.

---

[3] Art.3(2)(b).

The capacity of storage facilities

The Regulations impose requirements as to the capacity of storage facilities for livestock manure and other organic fertilisers, soiled waters and effluents from dungsteads, farmyard manure pits or silage pits. The capacity of such storage facilities must be adequate to provide storage of all such substances as are likely to require storage on the holding for such period as may be necessary to comply with the Regulations and the avoidance of water pollution.

Further, in complying with this obligation an occupier must have regard to the storage capacity likely to be required during periods of adverse weather conditions when the application of such materials is precluded.

The Regulations specify in detail the storage requirements required in respect of different types of livestock. Specific storage capacity requirements are prescribed for pig manure, poultry manure, manure from deer, goats and sheep, and manure from cattle. For this purpose, the country is divided into three zones detailed in Table 1 (see below).

The storage requirements are dependent on which of the three zones the holding is located in. The storage capacity required and the times when application of chemical fertilisers, organic fertilisers and farmyard manure is prohibited are set out in Table 2.

Exemptions to the storage capacity requirements

The Regulations provide for a number of exemption to the above storage capacity requirements: Holdings with in excess of 100 pigs must have 26 weeks storage in place by December 21, 2006. In all other cases, the relevant full storage capacity must be in place by December 31, 2008. Provision is made for reduced storage capacity in the following circumstances:

(a) In the case of pigs and poultry, generally there

must be 26 weeks storage capacity in place for pigs and poultry units; however, less storage capacity is required (the same manure storage requirement as applies for cattle in the relevant zone if:

(a) pig numbers do not exceed 100 at any time;

(b) poultry places are not more than 2,000; and

(c) the holding is big enough to take all of the livestock manure produced subject to the Regulations);

(b) In the case of deer, goats and sheep in certain circumstances for holdings with a stocking rate of less than 130kgs nitrogen per hectare a reduced storage capacity may be permitted to take account of outwintered livestock, and likewise with cattle which are outwintered at a grassland stock rate which does not exceed 85kgs nitrogen at any time during the period specified in Schedule 4 in relation to the application of organic fertiliser other than farmyard manure.

(c) In the case of organic fertilisers, reduced storage capacity is permissible where the occupier of a holding has:

(a) a contract giving exclusive access to adequate alternative storage capacity, located outside the holding;

(b) a contract for access to a treatment facility for livestock manure; or

(c) a contract with an authorised person or body who undertakes the collection, recovery or disposal of the manure.

Nutrient management

Part 3 of the Regulations deals with nutrient management and sets down fertiliser application limits for nitrogen and phosphorus. An occupier of a holding must take all such reasonable steps as are necessary for the purposes of preventing or minimising the application to land of fertiliser in excess of crop requirements on the holding. Organic and chemical fertiliser must not exceed the limits specified in the Regulations. The specified limits are set out in Schedule 2 of the Regulations and are based on individual crop needs.

Prevention of water pollution from fertilisers and certain activities

The Regulations contain a number of provisions designed to prevent water pollution from fertiliser and certain activities. These include legally binding limitations on the application of fertiliser and the imposition of restrictions on the application of fertiliser within specified distances from a water body, or watercourse.

The Regulations also impose requirements as to the manner of the application of fertilisers, and soil water, including requirements as to soil and weather conditions. In particular organic or chemical fertiliser must not be spread on land during the prohibited application periods set out in Schedule 4 of the Regulations. However, in recognition of the need for farmers to physically put in place the additional storage capacity required as a result of the enactment of the Regulations these provisions are subject to certain interim requirements.

Thus, as an interim measure, pending farmers having the required storage capacity in place, the prohibited period for spreading organic fertiliser (i.e. livestock manure) produced on the holding are the months of November and December, which is effective from August 1, 2006.

The organic nitrogen limit

The 2005 Regulations impose strict and severe limitations on the amount of organic nitrogen to be applied on a holding. In essence, for the purpose of the Regulations the amount of organic nitrogen is the nitrogen in livestock manure.

The key limit imposed by the Regulations is that the amount of livestock manure applied in any year to land on a holding may not exceed 170 kg of nitrogen per hectare and this limit is currently applicable. The Regulations set out in detail the basis for the calculation of these limits. The 170 kg limit applies to the "net area" of the holding.

The Department of Agriculture and Food itself has estimated that the average Irish dairy cow produces 85kgs of organic nitrogen per year and on this basis the 170kg limit is equivalent to 2 dairy cows per hectare and this stocking rate clearly brought many Irish farmers over the 170kg limit.

Following the publication of the Nitrates Regulations in December 2005 (described hereinbefore) there was a major furore created as the farming community revolted at the impact of the regulations as that would have extremely serious consequences for intensive dairy farmers, pig producers and those engaged in poultry production.

An intensive lobbying campaign was embarked upon, and with little progress being reported, the main farming organisations withdrew from participating in the Partnership talks.

This culminated in detailed and extensive discussions taking place between officials of the Department of the Environment, Heritage and Local Government, the Department of Agriculture and Food and Teagasc and the farming organisations, and significant amendments were made to the European Communities (Good Agriculture Practices for Protection of Waters) Regulations 2005, and these were submitted by to the Department of the Environment, Heritage and Local Government to the

European Union Commission on May 18, 2006. Eventually, the agreement of the Commission was secured to the proposed amendments, which basically provided farmers with greater flexibility in certain aspects while respecting the environmental requirements of the Nitrates Directive, and these new "Nitrate Regulations" which revoked and re-enacted with amendments the regulations made in December 2005, generally came into effect on 1st August 2006, with later commencement dates for certain provisions. Dick Roche, TD., the Minister for the Environment, Heritage and Local Government, in announcing the new Nitrate Regulations on July 17, 2006 hoped that the new regulations would be seen as a win-win outcome for Irish agriculture and for the aquatic environment.

The farming organisations, were more circumspect in their welcome, and requested the Department of Agriculture and Food, to consult with the farming organisations on the guidance that will be given to farmers who have to comply with, and implement the regulations.

The main new elements of the European Communities (Good Agricultural Practice of Waters) Regulations 2006, which is set out in full as an appendix in this book, because of its importance in the context of a framework to protect waters against pollution by nitrates from agricultural sources can be summarised as follows:

Transitional arrangements for manure from pigs and poultry

The prescribed limits for phosphorus and nitrogen fertiliser can be exceeded up to January 1, 2001 for lands using manure from pigs and poultry. No distinction will be made between licensed and unlicensed units. The overall 170 kg/ha. organic nitrogen limit will continue to apply.

Transitional provisions for REPS farmers

Application of fertilisers in accordance with approved REPS plans shall be compliant for the duration of the plan. New REPS plans will have to comply with the amended regulations.

Soil Phosphorus Index System

Teagasc phosphorus advice is based on a P index system and recommends the following approach to determining phosphorus fertiliser requirements –

1. Determine target P index for the soil based on intensity of stocking/production requirements.
2. Establish current P index of the soil (i.e. with a soil test).
3. Apply P fertiliser to bring soil to its target P index.
4. Apply P fertiliser to replace nutrients removed by crops and to maintain soil at its target P index.

Teagasc advice recommends a target P index of 3 on grassland for stocking rates equivalent to 170 kg organic N per hectare.

The amendments will revise Table 11 to the Regulations, which details the P index system, as follows –

Table 11: Phosphorus index system

Soil phosphorus index	Soil phosphorus ranges (mg/l) for grassland	
	Proposed new index	*Existing index*
1	0.0 – 3.0	0.0 – 3.0
2	3.1 – 5.0	3.1 – 6.0
3	5.1 – 8.0	6.1 – 10.0
4	Above 8.0	Above 10.0

The Regulations deem land to be at Soil P index 3 unless a soil test demonstrates otherwise. The Regulations do not require soil testing.

What does this mean? The amendments to the P index system reduce the cut-off points between soil P indices 2 and 3, and 3 and 4, and may increase the amount of land classified at the higher soil P indices. However, Minister Roche deemed this necessary to avoid any requirement to classify soils, as advised by Teagasc, in order to support the new target P index of 3 on grassland stocked at up to 170 kg org. N/ha.

Phosphorus fertilisation rates

The amendments will reduce the number of stocking rate bands in Table 13 from 18 to 4.

The Phosphorus fertiliser limits will be increased by 10 kg per hectare for P index 2 soils at stocking rates up to 170 kg org. N/ha., and 5 kg per hectare at stocking rates up to 210 kg org. N/ha. The proposed new Phosphorus table is as follows –

Table 13: Annual maximum fertilisation rates of phosphorus on grassland

Grassland stocking rate[1] (kg/ha/year)	Phosphorus Index			
	1	2	3	4
	Available Phosphorus (kg/ha)[2, 3]			
≤ 130	35	25	15	0
131-170	39	29	19	0
Grassland stocking rate greater than 170 kg/ha/year [4, 5]				
171-210	44	34	24	0
211-250	49	39	29	0

[1] Total annual nitrogen (kg) excreted by grazing livestock averaged over the net grassland area (grazing and silage area). Stocking rate refers to grassland area only.

[2] The fertilisation rates for soils which have more than 20% organic matter shall not exceed the amounts permitted for Index 3 soils.

[3] Manure produced by grazing livestock on a holding may be applied to Index 4 soils on that holding in a situation where there is a surplus of such manure remaining after the phosphorus fertilisation needs of all crops on soils at phosphorus indices 1, 2 or 3 on the holding have been met by the use only of such manure produced on the holding.

[4] The maximum phosphorus fertilisation of grassland shall not exceed that specified for stocking rates less than or equal to 170 kg/ha/year unless a minimum of 5% of the net area of the holding is used to grow crops other than grass.

[5] This table does not imply any departure from article 20(1) which prohibits the application to land on a holding of livestock manure in amounts which exceed 170kg Nitrogen per hectare per year, including that deposited by the animals themselves.

What does this mean? The reduction in the number of stocking rate bands provides some scope for increased flexibility in P fertiliser applications. In the absence of soil test results, soils are deemed to be at P index 3. The amended regulations do not provide for additional P fertiliser to index 3 soils. However, where soil test results indicate that soils are at P index 2, additional P fertiliser will now be allowed to build up soil fertility to the target P index of 3. The original regulations did not permit any additional P fertiliser on index 2 soils at stocking rates up to 170 kg per hectare.

Nitrogen fertilisation rates

The number of stocking rate bands in Table 12 will be reduced from 16 to 3, with increased nitrogen limits in line with Teagasc advice as follows –

Table 12: Annual maximum fertilisation rates of available nitrogen on grassland

Grassland stocking rate[1] (kg/ha/year)	Available nitrogen[2] (kg/ha)
≤ 170	226
Grassland stocking rate greater than 170 kg/ha/year[3]	
171-210	306
211-250	279

[1] Total annual nitrogen (kg) excreted by grazing livestock averaged over the net grassland area (ha) (grazing and silage area). Stocking rate refers to grassland area only.

[2] The maximum nitrogen fertilisation of grassland shall not exceed that specified for stocking rates less than or equal to 170 kg/ha/year unless a minimum of 5% of the net area of the holding is used to grow crops other than grass.

[3] This table does not imply any departure from article 20(1) which prohibits the application to land on a holding of livestock manure in amounts which exceed 170kg Nitrogen per hectare per year, including that deposited by the animals themselves.

Amendments will allow increased Nitrogen fertiliser

application at stocking rates up to the equivalent of 210 kg. org. N per hectare (or 1 lu/ac.) The increased N limits in the revised regulations will exceed those included in REPS plans.

Tillage

N index system for tillage crops: Table 10 to the Regulations details the Nitrogen index system for tillage crops. Tillage crops receiving frequent dressings of organic manure were classified as N Index 4, which significantly limited the amount of nitrogen fertiliser that could be applied to such crops, and acted as a disincentive for tillage farmers to apply organic fertilisers to their crops. This amendment will reclassify land receiving frequent dressings of organic manures from N index 4.

Increased nitrogen limits for certain crops (winter oats and milling wheat).

Ploughing and the use of non-selective herbicides: Article 21(5) is to be amended to clarify that a green cover crop can be grazed.

Other changes

- Statutory acknowledgement of integrated constructed wetlands, earth lined stores and out wintering pads.

- The level of available nitrogen and phosphorus is prescribed in relation to organic fertilisers other than livestock manure etc. (e.g. organic waste from industry).

- Provision is made for variation of the size of buffer zones around abstraction points for drinking water on the basis of site specific investigations.

- The date for completion of annual records is to be brought forward from June 30 to January 31 to facilitate DAF inspections for cross-compliance.

Schedule 1 (soil test) and other schedules are amended to clarify the meaning of "peat soils", i.e. soils with an organic matter content exceeding 20%.

New-age-categories for cattle are added to Tables 2 and 3 (Schedule 2) which increase the storage capacity required for cattle between 6-12 months and 17-24 months.

The provisions in relation to "continued offences" have been deleted.

The overall thrust of the new regulations will provide a new "transition period" which will clearly benefit pig, poultry and mushroom producers, and they would be well advised to utilise this period to acclimatise to this new regulatory regime.

Likewise there is a new transition period for REPS farmers, with revisions to the nitrogen index system for tillage crops, and a newly defined phosphorous index system for grassland. Finally, there is a reduction in the number of stocking rate lands for both phosphorous and nitrogen grassland fertilisation limits, and an increase in the nitrogen limit for grassland for the majority of farmers, when compared to the proposals in the December 2005 Regulations.

In addition to the organic nitrogen limits, restrictions were also imposed by the Regulations on ploughing and the use of non-selective herbicides. In simple terms, the regulations require that ploughing may only be undertaken at specified times and/or within specified time limits

Record keeping

One of the most important changes introduced by the Regulations arise from the record keeping obligations imposed. With effect from August 1, 2006, a series of detailed records must be maintained in respect of each holding. These records must be prepared for each calendar year by March 31 of the following year and must be retained for a period of at least five years. These records must indicate, amongst other matters the following:

• The total and net area of the holding;

• cropping regimes and their individual areas;

• livestock numbers and type;

• storage capacity on the holding;

• an estimation of annual fertiliser requirements for the holding; and the amounts of concentrates fed to grazing livestock,

The Department of Agriculture and Food has indicated that it will furnish farmers with an annual Organic Nitrogen Statement based on cross compliance records arising from the administration of the Single Farm Payments Scheme. However, individual farmers will still be obliged to calculate the organic nitrogen output for other livestock and add it to the statement figures.

Farmers who are already participating in the *Rural Environmental Protection Scheme ("REPS")* will be substantially compliant with the record-keeping requirements of the Regulations, arising from their REPS record keeping obligations. However it is envisaged that even farmers participating in REPS will need to maintain additional records recording the amount of concentrates fed to grazing livestock.

Offences

The failure to comply with the Regulations gives rise to a number of offences, which can result in a fine and/or imprisonment. Any person who contravenes the provisions of Parts 2 to 5 of the Regulations is guilty of an offence and is liable upon summary conviction to a fine not exceeding €3,000 or a term of imprisonment not exceeding six months or at the discretion of the court to both such fine *and* such imprisonment.

It should be noted clearly that in many cases the circumstances which give rise to liability for an offence under the Regulations (e.g. incorrect application of fertiliser resulting in pollution) would also give rise to liability under the water pollution legislation. It is likely that where a breach of the Regulations gives rise to a serious incident of water pollution, it is likely that the prosecuting authority would instigate criminal proceedings under the water pollution legislation.

The relevant County Council or the Environmental Protection Agency may take prosecutions for breach of the Regulations. The Regulations provide that the costs of any of any such prosecution, including the costs incurred in taking samples, investigations, etc. should be awarded to the County Council/EPA unless the court is satisfied that "there are special and substantial reasons for not so doing". It should be noted that the courts generally award such costs to the prosecution, and these costs typically exceed the fine imposed.

The administration and enforcement of the Regulations

The administration and enforcement of the Regulations is primarily the responsibility of the local County Council assisted by Environmental Protection Agency. Under the Regulations, County Council's and their authorised staff are responsible for the conduct of farm inspections to ensure compliance with the Regulations.

For this purpose, they are conferred with extensive powers of inspection and entry onto lands. These include the power (subject to certain conditions) to enter and inspect premises and conduct tests, surveys and if necessary remove evidence. They are also specifically empowered to inspect and require the production of documents and records.

However, it is envisaged that the vast majority of farmyard inspections under the Regulations are likely to be made by staff from the Department of Agriculture and Food under the cross compliance provisions of the Single Payment Scheme. These staff will of course be permitted to notify the relevant County Council where they consider there is non-compliance with the Regulations.

The Environmental Protection Agency will be responsible for the regulation of any intensive agricultural holdings, which are subject to an Integrated Pollution Prevention and Control ("IPPC") licence. It should be noted that individual farmers who import pig and poultry manure from holders of IPPC licenses may continue to operate under the terms of their current nutrient management plan until such time as it is subject to review by the EPA.

The relationship between the Regulations and REPS

The introduction of the Regulations initially gave to some uncertainty over the relationship between the Regulations and the Rural Environmental Protection Scheme ("REPS"). It has been suggested that arising from the introduction of the Regulations some REPS farmers would need to reduce their chemical nitrogen applications to conform with the requirement of the Regulations. However, the Department of Agriculture and Food considered that for most REPS farmers the practical impact of the Regulations would be minimal.

The Regulations are likely to require relatively minor

adjustments to current farming practice such as the storage of farmyard manure, restrictions on spreading periods and overall fertiliser limits, and the revised regulations have brought greater clarity to this area.

Table 1

Zones for organic fertiliser storage capacity requirements and prohibited application periods for organic and chemical fertilisers

ZONE A	ZONE B	ZONE C
Carlow, Cork, Dublin, Kildare, Kilkenny, Laois, Offaly, Tipperary, Waterford, Wexford, Wicklow	Clare, Galway, Kerry, Limerick, Longford, Louth, Mayo, Meath, Roscommon, Sligo, Westmeath	Donegal, Leitrim, Cavan, Monaghan

Table 2

Summary of zones, storage capacity required and prohibited application periods

ZONES	REQUIRED STORAGE CAPACITY	PROHIBITED APPLICATION PERIODS		
		Chemical Fertilisers	Organic Fertilisers	Farmyard Manure
A	16 Weeks	15 Sept-12 Jan	15 Oct-12 Jan	1 Nov –12 Jan
B	18 Weeks	15 Sept -15 Jan	15 Oct –15 Jan	1 Nov-15 Jan
C	20 Weeks	15 Sept –31 Jan	15 Oct –31 Jan	1 Nov -31 Jan
C*	22 Weeks	15 Sept – 31 Jan	15 Oct –31 Jan	1 Nov- 31 Jan

* These levels are applicable to counties Cavan and Monaghan

NOTE: Housed sheep, deer or goats must have six weeks storage capacity.

Water pollution

The law imposes significant controls on water pollution, which are of particular concern for farmers. These controls are contained in Water Pollution legislation and Fisheries legislation. The Local Government (Water Pollution) Acts 1977 – 1990, impose the most significant legal controls over water pollution. The provisions of the Fisheries (Consolidation) Acts 1959 - 1990 also contain significant controls over water pollution. These two statutory provisions operate in parallel, and although there is a degree of overlap, a situation that has arisen mainly by historical accident.

The Local Government (Water Pollution) Acts 1977-1990

Commencing in 1977 a series of Acts have conferred local authorities with extensive powers to maintain water quality and to prevent and mitigate the effects of water pollution within their areas. The principal provisions are contained in the 1977 Act, which was significantly amended in 1990.

This legislation creates a number of offences in respect of water pollution and makes provisions for penalties to be imposed on those responsible for offences under the Act. Farmers are frequently prosecuted under this legislation for the offence of causing water pollution.

The legislation also gives local authorities with extensive powers of prosecution of those responsible for water pollution. It also established a system of licensing for discharges to water and requires local authorities to prepare water-quality management plans.

Overview of the Water Pollution Acts 1977-1990

The Local Government (Water Pollution) Acts 1977 – 1990, applies to rivers, streams, lakes, canals, reservoirs, aquifers, ponds, watercourses or other inland waters, whether natural or artificial. Also included within the scope of the Act are tidal waters and, where the context permits, any beach, riverbank, salt marsh or other area which is contiguous to rivers, streams, lakes, etc. It is important to note that the wording of the Act is such that it brings within its scope polluting matter which is disposed close or adjacent to a water body in such a manner that it is likely that it will ultimately join the water body medium during a period of high flows or for some other reason.

As previously noted the Act, establish a system of licensing permitting the discharge of effluent into waters. Any such discharge is permitted provided it is in accordance with the terms and conditions of the licence. However, such licences are generally not applicable to agricultural activities.

Under section 15 of the 1977 Act, a local authority or two or more local authorities may make a water quality management plan in respect of any water situated in their functional areas or which adjoin those areas. The plan must contain such objectives for the prevention and abatement of the pollution of waters as appear to the local authority to be necessary. Plans may be subject to revision or replacement at the direction of the Minister for Environment or as the local authority sees fit.

Offences under the Local Government (Water Pollution) Acts 1977-1990

The Local Government (Water Pollution) Acts 1977 – 1990 create a number of offences in the context of water pollution. The principal offence under the Act is contained in section 3(1) of the 1977 Act. It provides that it is an offence for a person to "cause or permit any polluting matter to enter waters". The term "polluting matter" is widely defined. It includes any poisonous or noxious matter or substance which is injurious to fish, the food of fish or their spawning grounds, or is liable render such waters harmful or detrimental to public health or to domestic, commercial, industrial, agricultural or recreational use.

It will be noted that the definition of polluting matter is not confined to substances that are injurious to human health. Any substances that can cause damage to fish or aquatic life, could be considered 'polluting matter. Also covered are substances that may damage the recreational or tourism value of waters. Clearly a wide range of agricultural substances, such as slurry, or silage effluent or fertiliser run-off will fall within this definition. For this reason, substances which are non-toxic in their own right, e.g. milk, may in certain circumstances fall within the definition of "polluting matter" under the Act.

There are a number of defences to a prosecution under the Act section 3(1). It is a defence for the accused to prove that he or she took all reasonable care to prevent the entry to waters of polluting matter by providing, maintaining, using, operating and supervising facilities, and by employing practices or methods of operation which are suitable for its prevention. This defence, introduced by the 1990 Act, places an onus on the defendant to establish that suitable measures have been taken to prevent the entry of polluting matter into the water. A farmer who can demonstrate to the court that he/she has complied with Teagasc and other guidelines may be able to avail of this defence.

It is also a defence to a prosecution under the Act to prove that the entry of polluting matter into water was authorised by or under the provisions of a discharge license under the Act or an Integrated Pollution, Prevention and Control Licence (IPPPC) issued by the Environmental Protection Agency. In the context of agriculture such licences may be granted to some intensive pig or poultry farmers.

Enforcement and penalties

The enforcement of the Local Government (Water Pollution)

Acts 1977–1990 rests with local authorities and in certain circumstances with the Environmental Protection Agency. Prosecutions for an offence under the Act are generally taken by the local authority in whose area the waters concerned are situated. However, the Regional Fisheries Boards, may also take prosecutions under the Act. In certain circumstances private individuals who are affected in a particular way may bring a prosecution, although this is rare.

The Act confers extensive powers on local authorities to prevent or control pollution. These include the power to enter and inspect premises, to take samples, to serve notices and to take actions to prevent or control pollution. A local authority is also empowered to serve a notice requiring the termination of the entry or discharge of a polluting substance and the remedying of any effects. Where a person served with such a notice fails to comply with it, the local authority may take any steps necessary to secure the termination of the pollution and to recover the cost from the person served with the notice.

A person convicted on indictment of an offence under the Act may face fines of up to €31,743 and/or a term of imprisonment up to five years depending the gravity of the offence. Provision is made in the Act for a local authority to apply to the court to have any fine levied by the court paid over to it and a prosecuting authority may seek its expenses.

Civil liability for water pollution

The Local Government Water Pollution Act also imposes civil as opposed to criminal liability in respect of water pollution. In certain circumstances, the person responsible for water pollution under the Act may be required to compensate any person who has suffered injury, loss or damage as a result of said pollution.

Section 20 of the 1990 Act provides that where trade effluent, sewage effluent or other polluting matter enters waters and causes injury, loss or damage to a person or to the property of a person, the person may recover damages in respect of such injury, loss or damage. Damages may be recovered from:

(a) The occupier of the premises from which the effluent or matter originated unless the entry to the waters was caused by an "act of God" or an act or omission of a third party over whose conduct such occupier had no control, being an act or omission that such occupier could not reasonably have foreseen and guarded against; or

(b) any person who, by an act or omission, occasioned the entry to the waters which in the opinion of the court, would constitute a contravention by the person of a provision of the 1977 or 1990 Act.

Where the entry of trade effluent or sewage effluent is authorised under a licence, or where the entry of polluting matter to waters is exempted under section 3(5) of the Act, civil liability does not arise.

The control of water pollution under the Fisheries Acts 1959-1990

As previously noted water pollution is also regulated under the Fisheries Acts 1959 - 90. This legislation creates an offence of water pollution. The Fisheries Acts apply to any river, lake, watercourse, estuary or any part of the sea.

In essence the legislation provides that any person who throws, empties, permits or causes to fall into any waters any "deleterious matter" will be guilty of an offence. The term "deleterious matter" is for all practical purposes defined in the same manner as "polluting matter" under the Local Government (Water Pollution) Acts 1977 – 1990.

A prosecution may be taken under this legislation by the Garda Síochána, the Central Fisheries Board, a Regional fisheries Board, local authorities or any other person. Local authorities may take prosecutions under the Fisheries Acts, however in general they prefer to prosecute under Local Government (Water Pollution) Acts 1977 – 1990. In practice the vast majority of prosecutions under Fisheries Acts are taken by fisheries boards typically against farmers or local authorities.

A person convicted of an offence of causing water pollution under the Fisheries Acts may be liable of fines of between €1,700 to €31,745 and/or a term of imprisonment of between six months/or five years depending of the seriousness of the case. The prosecuting authority is generally entitled to its costs and expenses.

Distinction between prosecutions under the Water Pollution Acts and the Fisheries Acts

The provisions of the Local Government (Water Pollution) Acts 1977-1990 and the Fisheries Acts 1995-1990 are very similar in nature. However, there are two key distinctions, which distinguish the operation and enforcement provisions of the Fisheries Acts from those available under the Water Pollution Acts. Firstly, the Fisheries Acts do not provide an accused with a "reasonable care" defence and therefore it is more difficult to defend a prosecution under this legislation. Secondly, local authorities and sanitary authorities are immune from enforcement under the Water Pollution Acts, which is not the case under the Fisheries Acts.

Environmental issues

Under EU environmental law as given effect to in Irish law certain areas may be conferred as areas for special environmental protection. These designations are generally conferred as a result of the obligations of various EU directives such as the Habitats Directives, the Birds Directive. These designations can have a significant practical impact on farming. In addition the Planning and Development Act 2000 and Wildlife legislation permit certain designations to be assigned to areas of land. The main designations and their significance are summarised below.

Special Protection Areas

Special Protection Areas (SPAs) are areas designated for protection under the "Birds Directive" of April 2, 1979[4] on the conservation of wild birds. Under EU Law the government is obliged to ensure no pollution or deterioration of the habitats in such areas. Typically SPAs are located on estuaries, coastal areas or islands. Sites designated as SPAs enjoy protection under the Planning and Development Act 2000 and the Wildlife Acts 1976-2000. This means there are restrictions on the types of development and works or activities, which may occur in an SPA. In certain circumstances a licence for certain activities may be required.

Special Areas of Conservation

Special Areas of Conservation (SACs) are sites designated under the Habitats Directive of May 21, 1992[5] on the conservation of natural habitats and wild fauna and flora. Ireland is required to take appropriate measures to protect SACs and their habitats.

Many of these areas have been selected by the Irish Government and submitted to the EU Commission as part of a list of candidate SACs. This list of candidate SACs is being considered by the Commission, which may require the

---

[4]   Directive 79/409/ EEC.
[5]   Directive 92/43/EEC.

designated areas to be altered, or further areas to be added to the candidate list. The final list will be approved by the Commission and the Government will then designate the areas as Special Areas of Conservation. Whilst the process of designation of SACs is ongoing, all candidate SACs are protected as of the date of notification.

Sites designated as SACs enjoy protection under the Planning and Development Act 2000 and the European Communities (Natural Habitats) Regulations 1997. In practice this means there are restrictions on the types of development and works or activities, which may occur in an SAC. In certain circumstances a licence for certain activities in an SAC may be required. The fact that lands are situate within an SAC must also be taken into account where planning permission is sought.

Natural Heritage Areas

The Wildlife (Amendment) Act 2000 provides for the establishment of Natural Heritage Areas (NHAs) by Ministerial order, namely, areas which, on the basis of scientific evidence, are considered by the Minister for the Environment to be worthy of conservation by virtue of their special scientific interest for one or more species, communities, habitats, landforms or geological or geomorphological features, or their diversity of natural attributes.

Planning authorities are required to have regard to the integrity and conservation objectives of such sites when considering planning applications.

Special Amenity Area Order

Section 202 of the Planning and Development Act 2000 Act permits a planning authority to designate an area an Area of Special Amenity where the planning authority is of the opinion that by reason of the areas of;

(1) Outstanding natural beauty, or
(2) special recreational value and having regard
     to any benefits for nature conservation, an
     area should be declared an Area of Special
     Amenity.

An area may be designated an Area of Special Amenity by resolution of the planning authority or the Minister may direct a planning authority to make a Special Area Amenity Order (SAAO) in respect of an area on the basis of 1 or 2 above. An SAAO only comes into effect when confirmed and it may be revoked or varied. A planning authority may from time to time review an Order for the purposes of deciding whether it is desirable to revoke or amend the order.

The real significance of an SAAO Order is that both the planning authority and the Board must have regard to the provisions of the SAAO when considering a planning application. If a planning application relates to a development, which is in an area of Special Amenity this fact must be noted on the planning register. Invariably an SAAO order will operate to restrict the types of developments permitted in that area. In general it is more difficult obtain planning permission in an area designated as an SAAO.

Landscape Conservation Areas

Under section 204 of the Planning and Development Act 2000 Act a planning authority may designate "any area or place" as a Landscape Conservation Areas (LDAs) for the purpose of preserving the landscape. The effect of an LDA designation is that it permits planning authorities to effect planning control in the within the LDA in respect of developments which would normally enjoy "exempted development" status under the 2000 Act. In the context of the objective of landscape conservation, this would include activities such as the removal of hedges, ditches, or afforestation and land reclamation.

The 2000 Act sets out a detailed procedure of public consultation prior to the making of an order designating an area an LDA. The members of the Planning Authority having considered the proposed LDA and any submissions or observations of the public, may make the order (with or without modifications) or refuse to make the order. An LDA order may be revoked or amended and provision is made for public consultation in a similar manner to that outlined above.

Tree Preservation Orders

Section 205 of the of the Planning and Development Act 2000 Act provides that where a planning authority considers it expedient in the interest of amenity or the environment to make provision for the preservation of any tree, trees, group of trees or woodlands, it may for that purpose and for stated reasons, make a Tree Preservation Order with respect of any such tree, trees, group of trees or woodlands as may be specified in the order.

The 2000 Act establishes a procedure which must be followed where a planning authority proposes making a TPO. This requires the service of a notice on the owner and occupiers of the lands effected, the publication of a notice in a local newspaper. Submissions and observations are invited and must be taken into account by the planning authority before making the TPO. The planning authority may by resolution make the TPO with or without modifications.

A TPO may prohibit cutting down, topping, lopping or wilful destruction of trees. It is an offence to contravene a TPO or a proposed TPO. Breach of a TPO order result in fines of up to €12,697 or a period of imprisonment not exceeding two years.

A TPO may require an owner or occupier of land to enter into a management agreement in relation to the trees. Where such a management agreement is entered into a planning authority is required to provide assistance (technical and financial) towards such management.

CHAPTER 6

The Liability for Animals – A Never Ending Headache

Introduction

Over the centuries, because of the centrality of the role of agriculture, and in particular animal production as a source of income for so many in rural Irish communities, one is not surprised to find the evolution of a sophisticated set of rules pertaining to the liability that might arise in both a civil and criminal way for the owners of animals. A series of special rules were developed relating to animals, and as we all see the application of a particular rule depends upon a distinctive claim in law between wild animals and domestic animals, or what is now known in legal circles as "the *Scienter Principle*".[1]

The Animal – Domestic or wild – What liability?

Pursuant to this principle, if you had a domestic animal such as a dog, and it misbehaves in someway, for example by continually growling and stripping its teeth in an aggressive and threatening way, and exhibits what is called a "mischievous or vicious propensity", then if damage is caused, by that dog, the owner will be held liable. He will be so held only on the basis that he had knowledge that the dog in question had this vicious propensity, because he would clearly have exhibited the tendency on previous occasions.

---

[1]   See McMahon & Binchy, *Irish Law of Torts,* (3rd ed., Butterworths, 2000, Dublin), p.754.

So if a farmer has a collie dog pup, and over the years while rearing him, he notices that the young pup has an aggressive tendency to exhibit bad blood, by snarling or jumping up and growling at adults or children, then the farmer is clearly on notice that his dog is exhibiting a "vicious or mischievous propensity", and he will be held liable for any damage that this animal inflicts subsequently upon an innocent person visiting his premises.

A farmer therefore is clearly liable if the dog on his premises has previously bitten a person visiting the farm, or walking along the boundary road, for example, if the dog, as he will have had knowledge of the tendency or propensity of the dog from the previous incident. So the owner of a domestic or tame animal is only liable once he is aware, either by seeing the animal behave in this way himself, or being told by a member of his family or a neighbour of the fact that the dog *or* other domestic animal has a vicious propensity to do the damage of a kind, such as biting.

Where for example, the aforementioned collie dog on previous occasions did nothing more than hold out a paw, or lick a child, or jump up on a visitor to the premises, it is clear that such docile actions exhibited by the dog do not come anywhere near demonstrating a mischievous propensity, and if the same dog subsequently bites or injures a person or behaves in some way which is uncharacteristic, the farmer can in his defence to a personal injuries suit, plead that the dog on his premises had never exhibited such a vicious propensity before, and on the contrary had acted in a docile, loving and playacting way, and he could not have been on notice of this unusual subsequent behaviour.

A Court will pay particular attention to the evidence and circumstances of any such incident.

On the other hand, if a landowner keeps a wild animal on his premises, and if the wild animal inflicts damage upon a person who comes on to the farmer's premises, then the farmer is strictly liable.

So there is a clear distinction in law as to how liability is imposed upon a landowner, with respect to him having wild or domestic animals on his premises. Wild animals in Ireland would generally include, zebras, bears, lions and elephants, for example, but of course if one resided in another country, some of these could be classified as tame or domesticated animals. In this country, domestic animals include dogs, cattle, sheep, horses and cats.

The Control of Dogs Acts 1986 and 1992

It would be remiss not to consider the enactment of these important statutory provisions which now set out, inter alia, the principal rules pertaining to the civil liability for damage caused by dogs. These Acts did not abolish the prior right of a person to sue a farmer or property holder, where they suffer injury by being attacked by the collie dog, and the person attacked can show clearly that the particular dog had a vicious propensity as explained hereinabove, but these Acts offered a simpler alternative, and in the author's view, a less onerous route for a complainant to pursue a remedy, if they are the subject of injury by a dog

A perusal of section 21 of the Control of Dogs Act 1986, effectively imposes strict liability upon a dog owner, for any injuries caused by dogs to livestock, and for damage which results when a dog attacks a human being.

McMahon and Binchy in their excellent tome *Law of Torts*[2] have drawn attention to the difference of wording in section 21 in respect of how it imposes strict liability for injuries to the person only when there is an "attack" on a person by a dog, whilst in contrast, with regard to dogs and livestock, strict liability is imposed "for injury done by it to any livestock". Section 21 therefore reads as follows:

---

[2] *Ibid.*, p.759.

(1) The owner of a dog shall be liable in damages for damage caused in an attack on any person by the dog and for injury done by it to any livestock, and it shall not be necessary for the person seeking such damages to show a previous mischievous propensity in the dog, or the owner's knowledge of such previous propensity; or to show that such injury or damage was attributable to neglect on the part of the owner.

(2) Where livestock are injured by a dog on land on to which they had strayed, and either the dog belonged to the occupier of the land or its presence on the land was authorised by the occupier, a person shall not be liable under this section in respect of injury done to the livestock, <u>unless</u> the person <u>caused</u> the dog to attack the livestock.

(3) A person is liable in damages for any damage caused by a dog kept on any premises or structure to a person trespassing thereon only in accordance with the rules of law relating to liability for negligence.

    (a) Any damage or injury for which a person is made liable under this section shall be deemed to be attributable to a wrong within the meaning of the Civil Liability Act 1961, and the provisions of that Act shall apply accordingly.

    (b) Sections 11(2)(a) and 11(2)(b) of the Statute of Limitations Act 1957, shall apply to such damage."

It is noteworthy that in relation to a trespasser, it is clear from section 21(3) of the 1986 Act that if such a trespasser is injured by a dog, the ordinary principles of negligence apply, and strict liability is *not* imposed in this instance.

So section 21(1) imposes strict liability in respect of "damage" to the person and in respect of "injury" to livestock.

Section 21(4) applies the provisions of the Civil Liability Act 1961, to damage or injuries caused by dogs, and therefore section 34 of the Civil Liability Act 1961, pertaining to concurrent wrongdoers, and contributory negligence will, if necessary, be applied by the Court in the determination of liability of the issue before the Court.

There are other provisions in the Control of Dogs Act 1986, and Control of Dogs (Amendment) Act 1992, which deal with the control and licensing of dogs, and set out a procedure for dealing with stray dogs, and circumscribes the duties and responsibilities of local authorities, who are now empowered to employ dog wardens for carrying out inspections of premises where dogs are kept, and ensuring that dogs are licensed and kept under proper and appropriate control.

It would be foolish of the farmer or any dog owner not to keep any dog or other similar animal that is on their premises under proper control. If there is a chance that the dog shows a "vicious propensity", there is no substitute for ensuring that the dog is kept under control, and that members of the public are not exposed to such a dog.

If you have doubts about the temperament and propensity of your dog, you should consider having a muzzle placed on the dog when he is loose in or around your premises. This should only be placed on the dog under strict veterinary supervision and advice.

Cattle trespass

Where a farmer has cattle or sheep or horses or indeed goats or pigs on his farm, and if any one or all of them were to roam or stray of their own volition from the farmer's premises into a neighbours land for example, then according to the

Special Rule, the farmer owning the animals is liable, irrespective of negligence.

There is a subtle distinction which must be understood here, insofar as cattle which stray of their own volition on to a neighbour's property and possibly had to cross the road to do so, has the special rule applied to these circumstances and the owner farmer is strictly liable, irrespective of negligence, but if the same cattle were purposely driven by the owner farmer on to his neighbour's land, the liability is in trespass through the animals.

Trespass by way of animals therefore necessitates negligence or a deliberate act or intention on the part of owner farmer, whilst strict liability is imposed under the special rule of cattle trespass.

Driving animals on the highway – use reasonable care or otherwise common sense.

If a farmer brings his animals on to the roadway, and an accident occurs, the liability in respect of same will be determined in accordance with the general principles of negligence and nuisance.

Animals which are being driven on the public highway for the purpose of bringing them from one field to another should always be accompanied by at least two people and, if necessary, a dog which is properly trained for the purpose of controlling or shepherding the animals on the highway.

One of the personnel involved should be positioned well in front of the animals, and be taking steps by way of flag waving or hand signals or warning light to alert oncoming motorists or cyclists as to the presence of the animals on the highway. Similar steps should be taken by the person positioned at the rear of the animals.

Again it is common sense not to populate the whole road with animals such as to leave no avenue for vehicles to pass safely. Indeed it is the counsel of prudence nowadays, where farmers are moving large numbers of animals from one field to another, to move same by way of cattle transporter or lorry, and this is particularly so in the context of the volume of motor vehicles traversing our roads on a daily basis.

Wandering Animals: Duty of care and burden of proof

Up until 1985, if animals belonging to a farmer strayed on to the public highway and caused damage thereon, negligence did not attach to the landowners whose animals wandered on to the aforesaid road.

So prior to the enactment of the Animals Act 1985, the law that was applied to animals straying on to the public roads was as set out in the judgement given in the well known English case of *Searle v. Wallbank*[3] as follows:

> "An underlying principle of the law of the highway is that all those lawfully using the highway, or land adjacent to it, must show mutual respect and forbearance. The motorist must put up with the farmer's cattle and the farmer must put up with the motorist".

So, this was the law of the land which although set out in an English case, was followed faithfully in numerous Irish cases. It seems that this special immunity for straying animals was preserved until legislative intervention in 1985, apparently for the reason that to impose an obligation upon landowners to prevent cattle from straying on to the public highway was too onerous a burden for landowners, and in any event motorists on the public highway should take cognisance of the fact that they could encounter various obstacles in the course of their travel, including straying animals.

With one fell swoop, the Animals Act 1985, removed this

---

[3]   [1947] A.C. 341.

immunity and made farmers liable for damage caused by other
animals straying on to the highways, but the Act grounds
that liability in negligence principles.

So the fact that animals stray on to the public highway
constitutes prima facie evidence of negligence on the part of
their owner, but no more.

It is worthwhile to examine this important section of the
Act in great detail. Section 2 of the Animals Act 1985, states
as follows:

> "So much of the rules of the common law relating
> to liability for negligence as excludes or restricts
> the duty which a person might owe to others to
> take such care as is reasonable to see that damage
> is not caused by an animal straying on to a public
> road is hereby abolished.
>
> (a) Where damage is caused by an animal
> straying from unfenced lands on to a public
> road, a person who placed the animal on the
> land shall not be regarded as having
> committed a breach of the duty to take care
> by reason only of placing there if–
> > (i) The land was situated in an area where
> > fencing is not customary, and
> > (ii) he had a right to place the animal on that
> > land, and
>
> (b) in this sub-section, "fencing" includes the
> construction of any obstacle designed to
> prevent animals from straying, and
> "unfenced" shall be construed accordingly".

Although the landowners immunity was now gone, the
Section did not make the adjoining landowner strictly liable
in these circumstances. Indeed the Law Reform Commission[4]

---

[4]   LRC Working Paper No. 3 of 1997.

recommended the imposition of strict liability on landowners to restrain animals, but however the legislature in its wisdom decided not to impose strict liability and dealt with the matter as set out in the section hereinabove.

Burden of proof

In civil cases the burden of proof primarily lies upon the plaintiff who is alleging negligence against a defendant. However, in cases of negligence where animals stray on to the public highway, the presumption of "*res ipsa loquitur*" (the facts speak for themselves) shifts the burden of proof on to the defendant to show that he has taken all reasonable care to ensure that his animals will not cause damage by straying on to the public road and that there is no reasonable grounds or proof that he has failed to take such care.

Mr Justice Patrick Brennan, in the case of *McCaffrey v. Lundy*,[5] in one of the first judicial interpretations of section 2(1) of the 1985 Act, stated that he saw section 2(1) as creating a res ipsa loquitur presumption. It was his view, that where the plaintiff gave evidence that his motor vehicle collided with animals straying on the highway and was able to identify the owner of the animals, then there is a prima facie case to be answered by the landowner to rebut the presumption of negligence on his behalf.

This burden on the landowner is, of course, not one of strict liability, but in so far as he was concerned it was necessary for him to prove that he had exercised reasonable care, maintained the fences in a stock proof condition and taken all reasonable steps to ensure that his stock did not stray on to the public highway.

In so far as Mr. Justice Brennan was concerned in this case, any other interpretation or application of the onus of

---

[5]   I.L.T. (October 1998), p.245.

proof in cases like this would render the plaintiff's case impossible:

> "because of the impossibility of many situations
> of the plaintiff ascertaining the conditions of the
> landowners' fences which knowledge is peculiar
> to the landowner".

So the position after *McCaffrey* was, that once evidence was given in a case that a collision took place with animals which had wandered on to the public highway and the plaintiff was in a position to identify the owner of these animals, then there was a prima facie case to be answered by the landowner to rebut the presumption of negligence on his part and to prove on the balance of probabilities that he had taken such care as was reasonable to see that damage was not caused by these animals escaping from his lands on to the public highway.

This particular approach which has been seen was first enunciated by Judge Patrick Brennan in the District Court, was subsequently re-affirmed by Johnson J. in the High Court, in the case of *O'Reilly v. Lavelle*.[6]

In this case, action was taken by the plaintiff motorist who whilst driving after dark at about 10.00 p.m., collided with an animal, a Friesian calf. The animal was killed and the plaintiff's motor vehicle was severely damaged and he was claiming the cost of repairs and damages. The defendant claimed that the accident was caused by the negligence or contributory negligence of the plaintiff.

On the opening of the case, counsel for the plaintiff submitted that while he had not specifically pleaded the doctrine of *res ipsa loquitur* (the facts speak for themselves), he was entitled to rely on the doctrine provided his pleadings were adequate and the facts proved showed the doctrine to

---

[6]   [1990] 2 I.R. 372.

be applicable. Counsel for the defendant strenuously opposed this. Johnson J. stated as follows in relation to that case:

> "I am most surprised there is no reported decision in this important issue of straying livestock and I hold that the Animals Act 1985, has changed the law in this matter. The change which this Act has brought about was long overdue and I refer to the doctrine of *res ipsa loquitur* as stated by Erle C.J., as hereinbefore stated. District Justice Patrick J. Brennan was absolutely correct in his view of the law as above stated on the matter. Cattle properly managed should not wander on the road and therefore the burden of proof in this case shifts to the Defendant to show that he took reasonable care of his animals. I believe that there is no matter more appropriate for the application of the doctrine of res ipsa loquitur than cattle wandering on the highway".

Duty of care

It is clear, from a perusal of the foregoing cases, that the condition of the fencing and gates leading into a farmers premises are carefully considered by the Courts in order to determine whether the defendant farmer had exercised reasonable care in maintaining his fences in a stock proof condition and had taken all reasonable steps to ensure that his stock did not stray on to the public highway.

Indeed it is noted in the *McCaffrey v. Lundy* decision, that Judge Brennan held that a landowner in order to show that he took reasonable precautions, should not only bolt the gate on to the lands where stock are held, but must also securely secure the gate with a lock particularly if the lands are not in the immediate vicinity of the landowners house.

Indeed on a perusal of the analysis of the said judgement

by Margaret Cordial,[7] it is noted that she was of the view that the law on reasonable care had arrived at the position whereby gates leading from lands where stock were kept on to busy public highways should be kept locked at all times and that maintaining a lock on the gate would not be of any great inconvenience to a farmer.

It was noted that Judge Brennan in the *McCaffrey v. Lundy* case, considered that the gate in that particular instant case could have been easily opened by a child, a vandal, and a passer by, a person with a grudge or a severe gust of wind or even animals rubbing or scratching against the gate. He held therefore that because the gate in question was not locked, the defendant was guilty of negligence. He also found that the fencing not to be adequate in a number of places.

It would appear therefore from the principles enunciated in this case, in relation to the duty of care that the landowner is not only obliged to bolt the gates on to the lands, where stock are held, but also to fit gates with locks. It is absolutely of critical importance that fencing be maintained in a proper condition and it is clear that where such reasonable precautions have not been taken, that liability will attach to the landowner.

In the *O'Reilly v. Lavell* case, Johnson J. held that:

(a) that a number of animals had strayed on to the side of the public highway;

(b) that one animal (a calf) was killed when it collided with the plaintiff's motor vehicle which was badly damaged;

(c) that the rest of the animals ran across the roadway and up the laneway which divided the defendant's land;

---

[7] Margaret Cordial, BL, "The Duty of Care of Livestock Owners" as considered by the Supreme Court in *O'Shea v. Tilman and Enforced Holiday Farm Limited"*, *Bar Review* (June 1997).

   (d) the defendant was the owner of the animal in question;

   (e) that the onus of proof shifted to the defendant in these particular circumstances;

   (f) that the defendant failed to discharge the onus of proof that the fencing in this field was not defective in that his cattle escaped from and returned to this field on this occasion;

   (g) that it was highly improbable that some stranger opened the gate into this field and remained there, until the animals at their leisure returned, and he then closed it again.

In summary, all that is required of a farmer is to take reasonable care in respect of the fencing. Providing that he does this, liability will not be imposed upon him.

Eventually the Supreme Court got an opportunity to expound upon this area of law, when it had to decide upon an appeal against a High Court decision, in the case of *Patrick O'Shea v. Tilman Anhold and Horse Holiday Farm Limited*.[8]

In this case, the plaintiff was driving a motor vehicle along a public road, travelling from Bundoran in the direction of Sligo, when he collided with a horse which was owned by the second named defendant. It would appear that the first named defendant, *Tilman Anhold*, had a controlling interest in the second named defendant company, and it came to be accepted in the course of the trial that the horse in question was owned not by him but by the defendant company.

The plaintiff sustained quite serious injuries. In his judgement delivered on April 26, 1994, Costello J., (as he then was) found in favour of the plaintiff. He found that the second named defendant's were negligent, and that there was

---

[8] Unreported, Supreme Court, October 23, 2005.

no contributory negligence on the part of the plaintiff and the Judge awarded a sum in damages for injuries to the plaintiff as sustained. It was against this judgement, that the defendants appealed.

An agricultural consultant gave evidence that he was satisfied that the fencing was adequate for ordinary commercial horse purposes and he was of the view that someone must have let the horse out on the road. An equestrian expert had also testified that the only way the horse could escape was if someone had opened the gate and while he agreed that a horse could jump from three to seven feet, he stated he would be surprised if a horse would do so without being urged or forced.

In the High Court, the Trial Judge was faced with the question: in the circumstances were the owners of the horse liable to the plaintiff? He concluded:

> "The situation was that either the fencing on the laneway or field was inadequate or someone had opened the gate, let out one horse and closed the gate again. On balance the first possibility was much more likely than the second. The problem of dealing with fencing is a difficult one and the Defendant was unable to discharge the onus of proof on it. The Plaintiff was shown a breach of duty. There was no contributory negligence on the part of the Plaintiff".

On appeal to the Supreme Court, Mr. Justice O'Flaherty stated that there was no doubt that having regard to statutory provisions an onus rested on the defendants to show that they had taken reasonable care, but nonetheless that was the extent of the burden that rested upon them.

The defendants had proved that there was no negligence on their part through the evidence of their expert witnesses, insofar as the fencing was adequate, which testimony was not contradicted by the plaintiff's professional witnesses. They were not required to take the further step of proving how the animal came to be on the highway: whether through the act of a trespasser or whoever. The most that was required of a Defendant in this situation where the onus of proof rests on him is to disprove any negligence on his part. It is not as if this was a case of strict or absolute liability.

O'Flaherty J. continued:

> "The Learned Trial Judge approached the matter on the basis that one possibility was more likely than another; however, that, was not the proper frame on which the resolve the problem that was presented to him. A Trial Judge's essential task is to decide whether reasonable care had been taken by the owners of the horse in the circumstances of the case as required by the Act. The Judge, in effect, went close to imposing strict liability on the Defendants. This is to go too far. Legislation enacted in the future may provide for strict liability dispensing with the necessity to prove negligence, but that is not now the law. In any event, as between the two possibilities, I will regard the possibility that someone opened the gate and let the horse out as less unlikely than that that the horse cleared the fencing".

In the circumstances, O'Flaherty J. allowed the appeal.

Keane J noted that the defendants were the persons who brought the horse into the field that joined the highway and provided such fences and gates as were there.

Matters were, essentially under their control and the first element of res ipsa loquitur was present. As to the next requirement – that the accident was such as in ordinary circumstances would not happen if those who have the management used proper care, he noted that it was self evident that a horse will not normally escape from lands onto the public road if adequate fencing is provided and any gates are kept in a closed position. At the close of the plaintiff's case, there was, accordingly:

> "reasonable evidence, in the absence of explanation by the defendants that the accident arose from their want of care".

Keane, J., was therefore satisfied that the trial judge was correct in refusing to accede to the application for a non-suit made on behalf of the defendants.

However he went on to note that an explanation was offered by the defendants. The evidence of both the first named defendant and the experts called on his behalf, was that all the standard precautions in the way of fencing had been taken, and effectively therefore the horses did not stray on to the road due to inadequate fencing and that in their opinion that all reasonable care had been taken preventing animals straying on to the highway.

Keane, J., considered therefore that because of this explanation, the Trial Judge had erred in his reasoning when he went on to hold that it was more likely that the fencing was inadequate. He considered that even if the Trial Judge was satisfied as a matter of probability that the horse had managed to surmount the fence, it does not necessarily follow that this was due to any want of reasonable care on the part of the defendants.

Keane, J., considered that in cases where the Court is satisfied that the defendant has taken all reasonable care and precautions which ought to be taken by him to prevent an animal escaping, then the fact that the animal succeeded in escaping on to the road is not the result of any negligence on his part.

Farmers should therefore note that while section 2 of the Animals Act 1985, has abolished the old immunity from the law of negligence previously enjoyed by owners of land from which animals strayed on to the highway, it did not go so far as to impose strict liability or absolute liability on the farming community. Cordial in her excellent elucidation on the matter and having considered the implications of the *O'Shea v. Tilman* case, succinctly stated that the law in the matter would appear to be as follows:

(a) Where a defendant has brought animals on to land and where these animals stray from the land on to the highway, this constitutes a prima facie case of negligence.

(b) Where the defendant failed to adduce evidence to rebut the presumption of negligence on his part (i.e. that he had taken all due care to ensure his gates and fences were maintained in such a manner as to prevent animals escaping), the Court would be entitled to find against the defendant farmer in this case.

(c) Where, however, the defendant farmer can show that he has taken reasonable care to prevent animals escaping from his land, he is not required to take any further steps or prove how his animals came to be on the public highway.

(d) Where the court believes that reasonable care has been taken by the defendant farmer to ensure that his animals could not stray on to the public highway, and even if the animals still escape, the court is not entitled to find that this was due to want of care on the part of the defendant farmer. Once negligence is disproved, section 2 of the Animals Liability Act 1985 does not impose liability as it is not a case of strict liability.

(e) The court is not entitled to base its conclusions on the likelihood that one situation is more likely than another and to impose a finding of negligence on that basis. Even if one situation is more likely than another, this does not entitled the court to find that the defendant has been negligent.

Farmers nowadays are well in tune with the necessity of maintaining detailed records of their activities, such as stock numbers, the application of particular rates of fertilisers on their various fields and indeed for the purpose of general management.

In the author's view, details of the condition of fencing should be part of general management activity and indeed as part of their herding of their animals, they should pay particular attention to the maintenance of their fencing on their land. They should note the condition of same and where it appears to be aging or becoming inadequate or decrepit, steps should be immediately taken to replace same. A detailed note of the condition of their fencing should be entered into their records books and also where replacement of same takes place this should also be recorded.

Likewise where there is access to a farmer's field by way of gate which is located along the public highway, it is a counsel of prudence to have such gate locked with an appropriate padlock. This would ensure that the gate would not be opened by a child, or a passer by or indeed animals rubbing or scratching against the gate or by somebody who holds a grudge against the particular farmer. It would also go a long way in proving that he has taken reasonable care to prevent animals escaping from his land.

Such acts, such as placing a lock on a gate, might appear to be somewhat inconvenient and likewise recording various things in one's diary about the condition of a fence might likewise appear time consuming and possibly be over technical in nature. But ultimately one never knows the day or the hour when such attention to detail might prove to be very useful.

CHAPTER 7

Animal Health and Welfare

Disease control

Most people involved in the rural economy will be aware of the importance of animal health and welfare to their lives. Ask a member of the public about animal health issues and he or she will immediately think of the foot and mouth disease crisis in 2001; those over forty will remember the threat posed to Ireland by foot and mouth disease in the United Kingdom during 1968 and 1969. Some will be aware of the threat posed by BSE to the meat industry in the 1990's and others will be aware, in general terms of the continuing campaigns to control bovine tuberculosis and brucellosis in cattle.

The objectives of any disease control programme are, firstly, to minimize the risk of the introduction of a new disease, to prevent the risk of disease spreading and to control and eradicate indigenous disease.

There are two interconnected motives for controlling diseases of animals. The first is economic; animals that do not thrive and their produce will achieve a lower price than healthy animals or their produce if they are permitted access to market at all. The second motive is that some animal diseases cross the species barrier and have implications for human health; related to this is concern that animal diseases may be transmitted to humans[1].

---

[1] Historical overviews of disease control measures are given in D.Hoctor, *The Department's Story; A History of the Department of Agriculture* (Dublin, Institute of Public Administation, 1971) and M.E. Daly, *The First Department: A History of the Department of Agriculture* (Dublin, Institute of Public Administration, 2002) passim.

The legislative basis of our disease control measures can be traced back to Victorian times and, in particular, to the Diseases of Animals Act 1894. Some of the measures adopted under that Act may appear primitive and quaint to modern eyes.[2]

Nevertheless, the structures of that Act, albeit amended, remained in place until replaced by the Diseases of Animals Act 1966. That Act (as amended by the Disease of Animals (Amendment) Act 2001) remains one of the twin pillars upon which modern disease control measures are operated in Ireland.[3]

The second pillar underpinning disease control measures are various Directives, Decisions and Regulations emanating from the European Union. The greatest impact of these has been the introduction of the single market from 1992 with concomitant efforts to protect disease status by a combination of certification and non- discriminatory checks replacing a system where animal imports were prohibited save under license.

Both pillars of legislation are grounded in the scientific veterinary work of the World Organisation for Animal Health (usually known by its French initials - OIE), an international think tank founded in 1924 and based in Paris. The particular base from which animal health programmes are derived is the International Animal Health Code which is published and updated periodically by OIE since 1968. Because of their basis in the work of OIE, domestic legislation and EC legislation tend to have, broadly similar principles and policies and mechanics.

Generally, a disease will be notifiable.[4] A person having

---

[2] See the photograph published in Daly, *op. cit.*, showing people disinfecting in 1912; if nothing else, they were thorough.

[3] The Government has approved the drafting of a new Act dealing with animal health and disease control. The necessary Bill is in preparation within the Department at time of writing.

[4] Not all diseases affecting animals or, indeed, all animals are covered

suspicion of the existence of an animal disease must notify the Minister for Agriculture and Food (usually through the Department's local District Veterinary Office). The consequence of such a notification is that movement restrictions are imposed on animals and animal products from the suspect farm until the all clear is given. Movement is perceived as presenting a risk of spread of disease and this is borne out by the British experience in 2001. This will generally be as a result of veterinary surveillance carried out by veterinary practitioners who are civil servants in the Department of Agriculture and Food.

If the presence of a disease is confirmed, measures taken will vary according to the seriousness of the disease and may only affect the particular farm on which the disease is present. In the case of more serious diseases, movement of animals and animal products is restricted in a particular area and enhanced surveillance measures are put in place. Thus, during the 2001 foot and mouth disease campaign, the Cooley peninsula in Co. Louth was effectively quarantined from the rest of the country while movement restrictions were imposed nationally.

The most recent legislation dealing with notification and control of most animal diseases is the Diseases of Animals Act 1966 (Notification and Control) Order 2006.[5] This Order replaces over 30 measures dating back to the last century.

Certain diseases, in respect of which there are detailed regimes in operation, are made notifiable and the necessary controls implemented by specific statutory instruments made under either the Diseases of Animals Act 1966 or the European Communities Act 1972. Examples of these instruments are-

---

by the Diseases of Animals Act 1966. The up-to-date list is to be found in the Diseases of Animals Act 1966 (First Schedule) Order 2001 (S.I. No. 469 of 2001).

[5]   S.I. No. 359 of 2006.

(a) Bovine tuberculosis governed by the Bovine Tuberculosis (Attestation of State and General Provisions) Order 1989,

(b) brucellosis in cattle governed by the Brucellosis in Cattle (General Provisions) Order 1991,

(c) BSE governed by the European Communities (Animal By Products) Regulations 2003 and the European Communities (Animal By Products) (Amendment) Regulations 2006, and

(d) foot and mouth disease governed by the Foot and Mouth Disease Order 1956.

In certain cases, control regimes include the destruction of infected animals or animals at risk of being, or suspected to be, infected. If the Minister has an animal destroyed, compensation is payable. The general rule applicable is that compensation is payable at the open market value of the animal at the time of slaughter as if it were not diseased.

The regimes governing bovine tuberculosis and brucellosis are partially based on legislation and, in so far as compensation provisions are concerned, detailed administrative schemes negotiated with farm representative bodies. These are published annually and made available to farmers by the Department of Agriculture and Food.

As tuberculosis and brucellosis are the diseases that most affect Irish cattle farmers, it may be useful to summarise the main elements of the eradication schemes –

Tuberculosis

1. Eligible animals are tested annually and only animals that pass a TB test within the previous 12 months may be traded.

2. Reactors (i.e. animals suspected to be

affected with the disease) are culled. In certain cases, contact animals may be culled.
3. Movement restrictions are placed on farms where reactors are found; a farmer may move within his or her own holding or for slaughter under permit.

Brucellosis

1. All herds are tested annually and all female animals and bulls over 12 months must pass a blood test for brucellosis within 30 days of movement.
2. When there is an outbreak of brucellosis, all female animals in a herd are culled.
3. Movement restrictions are imposed prior to movement.
4. To prevent further outbreaks of brucellosis, a period of at least 4 months, must elapse prior to buying in. This period is determined having regard to disease risk.

As well as controlling diseases within Ireland, measures are routinely introduced to prevent the risk of disease being imported from abroad. These measures are usually giving effect to various European Commission Directives.

Thus, in 2006, the Minister for Agriculture and Food has made Regulations laying down the conditions for imports of products from Croatia, Bulgaria, Romania, Italy, Russia, Switzerland and Israel because of outbreaks of avian influenza. It is apposite to now examine the principal legislation which operates to safeguard animal health in the Republic of Ireland.

The governing law in this area is the Diseases of Animals Act 1966, as amended, and this provides the basic legislative code for the control and eradication of animal diseases. The First Schedule of the 1966 Act defines animals as cattle, goats, cats, dogs, horses, sheep and all other ruminating animals and swine.

The Act further defines poultry as domestic fowl, turkey, geese, ducks, guinea fowl, partridges, pheasants, grouse, pigeons, doves, pea fowl and swans. The categories of diseases of animals and poultry to which the Act applies are cattle plague, pleuro-pneumonia, foot and mouth disease, sheep pox, swine fever, epizootic, lymphangitis, parasitic mange, rabies, glanders, anthrax, fowl pest in any of its forms including Newcastle disease in fowl plague. Class B diseases include sheep scab, bovine tuberculosis, brucellosis in cattle and warble fly infestation.

Diseases that specifically relate to cattle include bovine leucosis, BSE, cattle plague, contagious bovine pleuro-pneumonia, lumpy skin disease and warble fly. The purpose of this chapter is to examine the major diseases that affect the national cattle herd, and in particular the significance of Bovine Tuberculosis and Brucellosis are examined.

The Diseases of Animals Act 1966

The central purpose of the 1966 Act is the prevention and eradication of disease in the national herds, and by doing so ensuring that the development of livestock production for both export and domestic markets will be aided. Further and to that end it is pertinent that we examine the powers of the Minister in relation to the prevention and eradication of the above listed diseases in the national herd. Section 13 of the 1966 Act provides that:

> "the Minister may, for the purpose of the prevention of checking or eradication of disease, make orders for all or any of the purposes set out in the Second Schedule".

There are a total of 22 purposes for which such an order may be made:

(1) An Order may be made securing and regulating effective isolation on land or premises and the prohibition or restriction of movement into or out of land or premises or part thereof of animals or poultry infected or suspected of being infected or capable of infecting animals or poultry with a disease.

(2) Securing and regulating the cleansing and disinfection of premises and removal therefrom and subsequent disposal of dung, litter, fodder or any other thing and exclusion of any animals and birds therefrom.

(3) Securing and regulating the cleansing and disinfecting of vehicles, places, pens, fittings and receptacles used for animals and poultry.

(4) Securing and regulating the repair or reconstruction of houses used for the housing of animals.

(5) Prescribing modes of cleansing and disinfection.

(6) Prescribing and regulating the marking of animals and poultry and prohibition of effacement, obliteration, alteration or removal of any such marking.

(7) Provides for the regulation of the seizure, detention and disposal of diseased or suspected animals.

(8) Securing a proper supply of water and food to animals during any detention.

(9) Regulating the destruction, burial, disposal or treatment of carcases of animals dying while diseased or suspected or slaughtered by a Minister for a local authority.

(10) Prohibition or regulation on the digging up of such carcases after they have been buried.

(11) Prescribing the regulation of disinfection of

clothes of persons coming into contact or employed about diseases or suspected animals.

(12) Prohibiting or regulating or restricting the sale, use or movement of any kind of fodder, litter or other material.

(13) Prescribing the treatment of diseased animals.

(14) Prohibiting the exposure for public sale or exhibition or the export of diseased or suspected diseased animals, except and in accordance with a licence.

(15) Prescribing and regulating the treatment to be applied in relation to any land for the purposes of preventing the spread of disease.

(16) Requiring the taking of samples of blood, urine, faeces or other bodily discharge, semen, saliva, milk, eggs, hair, wool, fur, feathers, mucus, skin or other tissue for the purposes of testing.

(17) Relate to such testing.

(18) Relate to such testing.

(19) Relate to such testing.

(20) Regulating or prohibiting the use of serums of vaccines for the treatment of diseased animals.

(21) Restriction on the business of dealing in animals or poultry unless authorised by licence to do so.

(22) Purposes ancillary or incidental to any of the foregoing purposes.

It can be seen from the foregoing extensive list of powers available to the Minister under section 13 of the Diseases of Animals Act 1966, that the prevention or eradication of disease, even forty years ago, was taken very seriously and assumed significant importance for the State. Given these concerns, schemes have been introduced with the similar objective of eradicating tuberculosis and brucellosis from our national herd.

One of the practical consequences of the existence of the schemes is that the national herd is tested annually and the Department of Agriculture, through its overarching role, attempts to ensure that such testing is as wide-ranging as possible. The further practical consequence of this in turn is that farmers are largely responsible for ensuring that arrangements are in place, and facilities are provided to enable this important herd test to take place.

Bovine tuberculosis

Bovine tuberculosis is governed by the Diseases of Animals Act 1966 and the Bovine Tuberculosis (Attestation of the State and General Provisions) Order 1989.[6]

Bovine tuberculosis is a highly infectious disease of cattle caused by mycobacterium bovis. This bacteria can cause disease in other domestic animals, in other wild animals and also in humans. The cattle become infected with bovine tuberculosis through the airborne transmission of the disease by already infected animals, or by the consumption of contaminated substances including water or through the sharing of farm machinery inter farm, and also from interaction with other animals. Article 3 of the Order of 1989 provides –

> "it appearing to the Minister to be necessary for the eradication of bovine tuberculosis and the Minister being satisfied that bovine tuberculosis is virtually non-existent in the State, for the purposes of such eradication and of the Act, the

---

[6]   S.I. No. 308 of 1989.

State is hereby declared to be an attested or a disease free area".

This declaration of the State as a disease free area is borne out by the statistical information below:

TB Figures 2004				
COUNTY	Number of Herds in County	Number of tests on Animals	No. of Reactors	Reactors per 1000 Tests APT
Carlow	1,458	113,301	208	1.84
Cavan	5,185	361,152	1,248	3.46
Clare	6,389	367,323	984	2.68
Cork NE	3,998	421,564	1,139	2.70
Cork Central	4,246	513,105	1,462	2.85
Cork SW	4,616	403,791	1,467	3.64
Donegal	6,049	229,406	403	1.76
Dublin/Wicklow	442	34,932	74	2.12
Galway	12,828	543,363	1,752	3.22
Kerry	7,337	437,143	800	1.83
Kildare	2,017	163,022	220	1.35
Kilkenny	3,320	416,804	1,075	2.58
Laois	2,974	277,262	451	1.63
Leitrim	3,355	116,310	392	3.37
Limerick	6,088	474,184	713	1.50
Longford	2,543	164,068	654	3.99
Louth	1,316	123,235	301	2.44
Mayo	10,831	351,147	612	1.74
Meath	4,030	437,723	1,010	2.31
Monaghan	4,363	276,010	877	3.18
Offaly	3,353	273,878	603	2.20
Roscommon	5,925	278,046	875	3.15
Sligo	4,005	162,964	428	2.63
Tipperary Sth	3,544	370,385	1,065	2.88
Tipperary Nth	3,570	413,089	945	2.29
Waterford	2,352	332,657	896	2.69
Westmeath	3,167	281,750	1,024	3.63
Wexford	3,393	322,852	777	2.41
Wicklow East	1,110	110,462	395	3.58
Wicklow West	610	54,792	117	2.14
TOTALS	24,414	8,825,720	22,967	2.6
Totals 2003	25,517	9,168,722	27,978	3.1

Report Date: 19/03/2006

			From	01/01/06		To	19/03/2006		
COUNTY	Number Herds in County	Number of Herds Tested	Herds Restr.	Herd Incidence Since 1/1/06	Herds Restr. on 19 /3/06	Number of Animals in County	Number of tests on Animals	No. of Reactors	Reactors per 1000 Tests APT
CARLOW	1,444	118	14	11.86%	35	93,829	11,334	70	6.18
CAVAN	5,154	579	28	4.84%	116	225,349	38,764	138	3.56
CLARE	6,371	542	18	3.32%	106	284,044	33,398	89	2.66
CORK Central	3,993	386	17	4.40%	88	336,450	46,183	89	1.93
CORK North	4,274	368	24	6.52%	122	380,600	44,840	73	1.63
CORK West	4,524	528	39	7.39%	161	287,109	49,712	160	3.22
DONEGAL	5,848	579	31	5.35%	118	177,900	31,220	80	2.56
DUBLIN	443	39	5	12.82%	20	24,007	3,995	8	2.00
GALWAY	12,570	964	51	5.29%	238	417,347	48,927	318	6.50
KERRY	7,268	470	20	4.26%	91	346,939	34,834	106	3.04
KILDARE	2,035	242	9	3.72%	48	122,273	23,928	49	2.05
KILKENNY	3,314	379	25	6.60%	100	314,943	52,207	50	0.96
LAOIS	3,011	406	23	5.67%	73	232,571	39,417	71	1.80
LEITRIM	3,337	247	13	5.26%	49	76,048	12,220	68	5.56
LIMERICK	5,893	438	24	5.48%	118	399,275	46,092	120	2.60
LONGFORD	2,531	390	34	8.72%	119	117,195	25,131	263	10.47
LOUTH	1,268	123	10	8.13%	35	82,664	11,340	17	1.50
MAYO	10,662	508	23	4.53%	70	266,735	23,223	40	1.72
MEATH	4,028	603	37	6.14%	170	279,451	65,089	123	1.89
MONAGHAN	4,370	540	32	5.93%	109	202,168	35,780	158	4.42
OFFALY	3,282	282	17	6.03%	85	219,339	31,530	57	1.81
ROSCOMMON	5,875	452	19	4.20%	108	197,042	26,598	84	3.16
SLIGO	3,996	320	10	3.13%	49	114,811	17,635	51	2.89
TIPP NORTH	3,497	540	33	6.11%	132	295,957	56,681	177	3.12
TIPP SOUTH	3,554	337	21	6.23%	116	304,606	39,849	119	2.99
WATERFORD	2,364	318	23	7.23%	86	237,212	39,634	179	4.52
WESTMEATH	3,125	410	31	7.56%	147	199,943	42,112	147	3.49
WEXFORD	3,312	510	41	8.04%	125	252,844	51,756	127	2.45

WICKLOW E	1,125	131	11	8.40%	35	75,664	12,461	48	3.85
WICKLOW W	612	75	5	6.67%	12	40,880	8,578	8	0.93
TOTALS	**123,080**	**11,824**	**688**	**5.82%**	**2,881**	**6,605,195**	**1,004,468**	**3,087**	**3.07**

Article 6(1) of the Bovine Tuberculosis (Attestation of the State and General Provisions) Order 1989 is instructive, and needs to be considered in full, as it sets out in comprehensive and all embracing detail the procedures to be adopted for the TB test. It states that:

> "The following provisions shall have effect in relation to the tests:
>
> (a) The test to be used to be the single comparative intradermal tuberculin test using PPD Weybridge bovine and avian tuberculins or a test specified in an authorisation in writing by the Minister which is for the time being in force;
>
> (b) The test shall be carried out by a <u>registered veterinary surgeon;</u>
>
> (c) The whole of the test shall be carried out by the same veterinary surgeon, except where otherwise authorised by a veterinary inspector, and the test shall be commenced and completed on the same holding;
>
> (d) The test shall not be carried out in circumstances which might affect its accuracy;
>
> (e) The owner or person in charge of an animal proposed to be or being tested shall inform the veterinary surgeon carrying out the test of the existence of any circumstances of which he may be aware including the previous use or application of Johnin which

might affect the accuracy of the test;

(f) Each site of which tuberculin is injected shall, immediately before the injection of the tuberculin be closely clipped over an area which is not less than enclosed by a circle of 2.5cm. (1 inch) diameter;

(g) On the day which the test is commenced, the veterinary surgeon carrying out the test shall send a notice of the test by post to the veterinary inspector in charge of the District Veterinary Office in the area in which the test is carried out;

(h) If the animal being tested does not already bear an approved ear tag the following provisions shall be complied with;

   i.   The veterinary surgeon carrying out the test shall, at the commencement of the test attach an approved ear tag to the left ear of the animal concerned,

   ii. Such approved ear tag shall bear the identification letter appropriate to the county in which the test is carried out and a serial number, and,

   iii. The owner or person in charge of the animal shall permit such approved ear tag to be so attached;

(i) Prior to the commencement of any test the owner or person in charge of the animal or animals proposed to be tested shall surrender to the veterinary surgeon who is carrying out the test every identity card issued in respect of any animal on the holding on which the test is proposed to be carried out;

(j) (i) Where a test, other than a test authorised under paragraph 2 of this article, is carried out and the owner or a person in charge of a holding omits to present for testing all the animals for the time being on the holding on which the test is carried out, the omission by him is hereby declared to be an offence,

(ii) prior to the commencement of any test the owner or person in charge of the animal or the animals intended to be tested shall, if required by a veterinary inspector or an authorised officer intending to carry out the test, make a declaration in writing in the form specified in the First Schedule to this Order;

(k) The veterinary surgeon carrying out the test shall report the result thereof to the District Veterinary Office in the area in which the test was carried out without delay in such form as may be directed by or on behalf of the Minister from time to time and attach thereto any declaration made (if any) under article 5(2) of this Order or under subparagraph (j) (ii) of this paragraph;

(l) Where in the opinion of the veterinary surgeon who carried out the test an animal tested has given a positive result the veterinary surgeon shall forward to the District Veterinary Office in the area in which the test is carried out with his report under sub-paragraph (k) of this paragraph, all the identify cards surrendered to him in accordance with sub-paragraph (i) of this paragraph;

(m) Where in the opinion of the veterinary surgeon who carried out the test none of the animal's tests has given a positive or inclusive result, the veterinary surgeon shall endorse each of the identity cards surrendered to him in accordance with the said sub-paragraph (i) with an indication that the animal concerned has passed the test and return the identity cards, when duly endorsed, to the owner or person in charge of the holding on which the test was carried out;

(n) Where, in the opinion of the veterinary surgeon who carried out the test, none of the animals tested has given a positive result but the result of the test has as regards any animal, animals, being inconclusive, the veterinary surgeon shall –

(i) Forward to the District Veterinary Office in the area in which the test was carried out, with his report under sub-paragraph (k) of this paragraph the identity card of each animal as respects which the results of the tests was, in his opinion, inconclusive, and

(ii) Endorse each of the remaining identity cards surrendered to him in accordance with sub-paragraph (i) of this paragraph with an indication that the animal concerned had passed the test and returned those identity cards, when duly endorsed to the owner or person in charge of the holding on which the test was carried out".

The obligations imposed by this section on the farmer are as follows:

1.   At paragraph (e) the owner or person in

charge of the animal must inform the surgeon carrying out the test of any circumstances which may affect the veracity the test.

2. The owner or person in charge of the animal must surrender every identity card issued by the Minister pursuant to this Order.

3. Where a test has been authorised the owner or person in charge of a holding must present all animals for the time being on the holding. Failure to do so is an offence at law.

4. The owner or person in charge of an animal or animals may be required to make a written declaration that all animals in his possession or under his control have been presented and that all identity cards have been surrendered to the testing veterinary surgeon.

As outlined in the decision of the High Court in *Carroll v. The Minister for Agriculture and Food*,[7] Blayney J. then of the High Court stated:-

> "Where a veterinary inspector is satisfied or has reasonable grounds for suspecting that there is a reactor on the holding or bovine tuberculosis is present on the holding, the article obliges him to declare the holding to be a restricted holding. He has no discretion in the matter".

The obligations imposed on the veterinary surgeon who carries out the test pursuant to Statutory Instrument Number 256 of 1978, ensure that the veterinary surgeon has no discretion. Those obligations can be summarised as follows;

• To report the results of the test carried out to the district veterinary office.

---

[7]   [1991] 1 I.R. 230.

- If the veterinary surgeon is of the opinion that the animal tested has produced a positive result the veterinary surgeon shall forward to the district veterinary office in the area in which the animal was tested a report and all identity cards furnished.

- Where in the opinion of the veterinary surgeon none of the animals have tested positive, the veterinary surgeon shall endorse each identity card surrendered and duly return identity cards to the farmer.

- Where inconclusive results are returned, the veterinary surgeon must forward a report to the district veterinary office.

In *Carroll v. The Minister for Agriculture and Food*, there is an illuminating judicial response to the plaintiff's application that a declaration under article 12 of the Order (dealing with the declaration of a holding as a restricted holding where a reactor has been found on that holding), lacked basic fairness, Blayney J. stated:

> "The question is whether, given the importance in the public interest of eradicating bovine tuberculosis, article 12 of the Order lacks basic fairness. It seems to me that it does not. Strict measures are necessary. To permit an appeal against the test findings of a veterinary surgeon would introduce delays into the scheme which could jeopardise its effectiveness to identify, isolate and remove reactors. Furthermore, the tests are conducted by an independent veterinary surgeon, the manner in which they are to be carried out is laid down strictly in the Order and the risk of error in any test result would appear to be slight, since all that is involved in ascertaining the result of a test is a physical

measurement with a calibre. In the circumstances
I am satisfied that there is not any want of basic
fairness and that the Order is not defective".

Compensation regime for bovine tuberculosis

The main schemes in the compensation regime for
compensation are:

- The on farm market valuation scheme,

- the income supplement scheme,

- the depopulation grant scheme, and

- the hardship grant scheme.

In order to qualify for payment the owner or person in charge
must meet certain eligibility conditions under each scheme.
Each scheme requires compliance with both the Diseases of
Animals Act 1966 and any regulations made thereunder and
also specifically the Bovine Tuberculosis Order of 1978.

The Minister may refuse payment of compensation in
whole or in part where the owner or person in charge does
not satisfy the requirements or where the Minister is satisfied
that that person has failed to cooperate with the authorised
officers or veterinary inspectors in carrying out their duties
and obligations under the scheme.

Income supplement

Income supplement is payable in cases where disease break
down results in the removal of more than 10% of animals in
the herd and where depopulation is not deemed appropriate.
Payment is in respect of each animal removed as a reactor
from the herd, subject to a maximum of 100 qualifying for
payment.

Quantification

Tuberculosis Income Supplement Quantity Rates from January 1 to December 31, 2005 for dairy cows and other animals both pedigree and non-pedigree was €25.39 and for other cows was €38.09. This income supplement is not available where the herd is totally or partially depopulated.

In circumstances where the herd is depopulated the tuberculosis depopulation grant rates are: for dairy cows in calf, heifers and pedigree bulls under 12 months of age was €57.13 per month for pedigree and non-pedigree animals, for other cows and in-calf heifers €31.74 a month and for all other animals €19.04 per month.

Further if the compensation payment exceeds €6,500 in a 12 month period a tax clearance certificate is required.[8]

It is to be noted at this stage that entitlements to compensation under the Bovine Tuberculosis Eradication Scheme and the Diseases of Animals Act 1966, and the regulations made thereunder, is not an absolute right.

While there has been some litigation concerning the disease programmes, most of the relevant litigation has concentrated on individual matters relating to or pertaining to compensation or how an individual was actually treated by the Department of Agriculture and Food, and there has been remarkably little law affecting areas other than compensation.

Nevertheless, a significant judgement was given in the decision of the Supreme Court in the case of *Rooney v. The Minister for Agriculture and Food*,[9] wherein, the Supreme Court held that the administrative scheme which the Minister for Agriculture and Food put in place vindicated the plaintiff's

---

[8] Further information regarding disease eradication schemes can be obtained from the ERAD Division of the Department of Agriculture and Food, Maynooth Business Campus, Maynooth, County Kildare or from each of the Department's District Veterinary Offices.

[9] [1991] 2 I.R. 539.

property rights whilst the plaintiff had contended that if the compensation scheme was placed on a statutory footing he would have gained significantly from it from a financial viewpoint.

The factual background to the *Rooney (No. 1) case* was that in 1984, 20 of the plaintiff's cattle were slaughtered pursuant to the Bovine Tuberculosis (Attestation of the State and General Provisions) Order 1978, then in force, as they were reactors. The plaintiff was paid certain monies by the first named defendant (the Minister) in respect of these animals pursuant to an extra-statutory scheme which the Minister had established. In 1985, a further 26 animals were slaughtered. No monies were paid in respect of these as the plaintiff had failed to comply with certain conditions set out in the extra-statutory scheme. The plaintiff issued proceedings claiming that he was entitled to compensation in accordance with the provisions of the Act of 1966 as opposed to the payment of grants pursuant to the extra-statutory scheme.

The proceedings in *Rooney (No. 1)* took an unusual turn. On an appeal from an Order of the High Court striking out the claim against certain of the parties named as defendants, the Supreme Court directed that the proceedings against all save the Minister for Agriculture and Food, the Minister for Finance, the Taoiseach, Ireland and the Attorney General be stayed pending the determination of the substantive issue of law raised in the claim being resolved in the High Court by way of the "special" procedure pursuant to Order 34 of the Rules of the Superior Courts 1986.

This Order provided that if it appears to the Court that there is in any cause or matter a question in law which it would be convenient to decide before any evidence is given or any question of fact is tried, the Court may direct such questions of law to be raised for the opinion of the Court by special case and all such further proceedings as the decision of such question of law may render unnecessary, may thereupon be stayed.

The issues raised and tried in the special case were the following claims by the plaintiff:

    (1) Where the declaratory judgment or Order that the plaintiff was legally and constitutionally entitled to compensation under and in accordance with the Act of 1966 and in accordance with the 1978 Order and that the court grant him the remedy or relief of exemplary damages or whatever relief the court shall think fit; and

    (2) The system of grant payments is operated by the Minister in his implementation of the Act of 1966 to the disease eradication schemes was unconstitutional when used as an alternative to compensation or in a manner that failed to comply with the compensation provisions of the Constitution; and that the self disposal of reactor animals as per the direction of the Minister does not diminish a herd owner's legal and constitutional right or entitlement to compensation or relieve the Minister of his duty to honour and safeguard such entitlement.

The plaintiff's claims were dismissed in the High Court.

The provision of the Act of 1966 which were primarily considered by the Supreme Court were sections 20, 22 and 58. It was clear that bovine tuberculosis fell into the class B category and section 19 empowered the Minister, where it appeared to him to be necessary for the purpose of eradication of any class B disease to make Orders, *inter alia*, declaring an area in which he is satisfied that the disease is virtually non-existent, to be an attested or a disease free area.

In the 1978 Order, the State as a whole was declared to be an attested or a disease free area. Section 20 empowered the

Minister to make, in relation to an attested or a disease free area, an Order including –

> "(a) As to animals... affected or suspected of being affected or capable of affecting animals... with the relevant disease –
>   (i) authorising the taking and possession, by agreement of the animals ... on behalf of the Minister;
>   (ii) in default of agreement, securing or regulating the removal out of the area or slaughter of the animals...
>   (iii) securing or regulating the isolation and maintenance of the animals... pending their been taken possession of on behalf of the Minister or removed out of the area or slaughtered".

Section 22 provided that the Minister shall, subject to section 58, pay compensation for animals taken possession of on his behalf pursuant to an Order under section 20. Section 58 provided that the section shall apply in relation to compensation under, *inter alia*, section 22.

Section 58(2) provided as follows:-

> "The Minister, with the consent of the Minister for Finance, may by Order:
> (a) Make provision for regulating the making and determination of applications for, and the mode of assessment and payment of, compensation;
> (b) Include provision for the fixing of compensation by agreement between the applicant and the Minister, or, in default of agreement, by a valuer appointed by agreement between the applicant and the

> Minister, or, in default of such agreement,
> by a valuer appointed by the Minister;
> (c) Include provision, in the event of the
>   applicant disputing the determination of the
>   application, for the settlement of the dispute
>   by arbitration."

When *Rooney (No. 1)* was being prosecuted no regulations
had been made by the Minister under section 58.

The respective positions of the plaintiff and the Minister
on the appeal in *Rooney (No. 1)* were summarised as follows
by O'Flaherty J., (with whom McCarthy and Egan JJ.,
concurred), in the following passage in his judgment:-

> "The plaintiff's case, put simply is that (the Act
> of 1966) provides the relevant machinery to
> enable him to receive compensation if the
> Minister would only activate the relevant
> provisions. The Minister's stance is that while
> he has put in place a system of grant payments
> subject to compliance with conditions contained
> in the scheme, these grants are separate from his
> entitlement to pay "compensation" under the Act
> of 1966 and he is not obliged to activate the
> compensation provisions of the Act".[10]

The plaintiff submitted that if section 58 was in operation
then he would fare better by being able to seek agreement
with the Minister for the fixing of compensation by, if
necessary, having a valuer appointed by agreement between
the Minister and himself or, in default of agreement, by a
valuer appointed by the Minister or by a process of arbitration
pursuant to section 58(2)(b) and (c).

This, he submits would be more beneficial to him than

---

[10] [1991] 2 I.R. 539 at 543.

the extra-statutory scheme which involves a unilateral element which means that the herd owner may have to take or leave what is on offer by way of grants as opposed to the more beneficial regime that would be in operation if there was a process of dialogue in seeking agreement between the parties and, ultimately, the possibility of resort to arbitration. This, of course involved not only that the Minister should bring into operation section 20, but that he should also "by agreement" take possession of the diseased animals.

The Minister's response to the plaintiff's submissions were summarised by O'Flaherty J., follows:-

> "On behalf of the Minister it has been submitted that this scheme operates better to safeguard public funds and if the Minister were to take possession of cattle under section 20 he would be likely to fare less well financially than a herd owner who would bring his cattle directly to those conducting the factory carrying out slaughtering operations – human nature being what is".[11]

O'Flaherty J., concluded that if section 20 and section 58 were in operation it would be vastly more expensive than the scheme then currently in operation which itself was *"a huge cost to the exchequer"*. When stated that this was at least a plausible reason for the operation of the extra-statutory scheme, he continued:

> "The Court will only be entitled to review such a decision on a course of action (embodied in the scheme) if it were satisfied that the decision and course of conduct was mala-fides – or, at

[11] *Ibid.*, p. 546.

the least, that it is involved in an abuse of powers: (see *Pinevalley Developments v. The Minister for the Environment* [1987] I.R. 23). It may be that the Court has no power to enjoin the Minister to make Orders under section 20 (C.F. the *State (Sheehan) v. The Government of Ireland* [1987] I.R. 550), in any circumstances but it certainly has no power to do so in the absence of proof of mala-fides or abuse of power".

O'Flaherty J., held that the Minister was not obliged to operate the Act of 1966 since he had in place "a reasonable scheme for providing a measure of assistance to herd owners of diseased cattle".

On the basis of so holding, O'Flaherty J., held that it was not necessary to enquire into whether there is any constitutional requirement to provide compensation for herd owners who have diseased animals. However, he added the following *obiter dictum*:-

"In any event, assuming that there is a constitutional requirement to provide for compensation in such circumstances, the Minister would only be obliged to act to provide compensation as far as practicable, having regard to the common good and that means that he should act in accordance with the advice that he get and having regard to other claims on public funds. Clearly he has, by the scheme in operation, in effect provided for this".

The Supreme Court dismissed the plaintiff's appeal.

It is suggested therefore that in the light of the foregoing outcome, albeit an *obiter dictum*, the Minister once he is providing compensation, has only to do so as far as practicable, and the impact of any such compensation scheme must be viewed having regard to the common good and more significantly having regard to other claims on the public funds.

Down on the farm many farmers who find themselves the subject of depopulation Orders can often complain bitterly at the level of compensation afforded them and more particularly where there are pedigree animals involved. Sometimes farmers feel in a moment of compulsiveness or reaction, that they should pursue this issue through the courts and have their arguments for an appropriate compensation scheme put in place which would reflect the actual replacement value of the very valuable stock that they would be losing from their herd which impacts adversely not only on the current year production, but very often for a significant period into the future. If one examines the *Rooney* decision carefully, the chances of launching such a successful claim are extremely remote and probably futile at this point in time.

Brucellosis

Brucellosis in cattle is governed by the Diseases of Animals Act 1966, and the Brucellosis in Cattle (General Provisions) Order 1991.

Brucellosis is a bacterial disease caused by a group of related bacteria known as the brucella species. It can be further divided into four separate sub-categories. Each of these four categories have their preferred host, but each can infect and do infect a wide range of animals and humans. In cattle, brucella abortus is the principle cause of brucellosis, and transmissions to humans can occur by consuming unpasteurised milk or dairy products and by direct contact with an infected animal or with contaminated material.

The disease in cattle is characterised by abortion laden pregnancy after which a degree of immunity develops. Infected cattle do not eliminate the bacteria from their system. Transmission of the disease may occur by ingestion of the bacteria often through drinking unpasteurised milk from infected cows, inhalation, exposure to bacteria in trees, can also be transmitted through the skin, and because of their occupations farmers, farm workers, veterinarians, meat factory workers, butchers and laboratory staff may periodically be exposed to infection.

Brucellosis position on 31/12/05									
	Current					Year to Date			
DVO	Total herds 31/12/05	Current Reactor Herds	Herds with 2 or more clear tests	Net Restricted Herds		Herds Depop. 2005	Herds with new 2005 restrictions	R+ animals 2005	In contacts removed 2005
Donegal	5,898	0	0	0		0	0	0	0
Galway	12,564	0	0	0		0	3	3	0
Leitrim	3,342	3	0	3		1	2	2	161
Longford	2,541	0	0	0		0	1	1	0
Mayo	10,660	0	0	0		0	4	4	0
Roscom.	5,887	1	0	1		1	6	2	39
Sligo	3,997	1	0	1		0	2	2	0
Sub-total	**44,889**	**5**	**0**	**5**		**2**	**18**	**14**	**200**
Cavan	5,153	2	0	2		1	5	6	91
Dublin+Ze	1,571	1	0	1		0	2	2	0
Louth	1,283	0	0	0		0	1	1	0
Meath	4,032	3	2	0		1	7	6	15
Monaghan	4,374	1	0	1		1	2	2	57
Offaly	3,283	7	3	3		1	10	8	156
Westmeath	3,129	0	0	0		0	2	1	0
Sub-total	**22,825**	**14**	**5**	**7**		**4**	**29**	**26**	**319**
Carlow	1,450	0	0	0		0	5	4	0
Kildare+Zw	2,661	0	0	0		0	4	4	0
Kilkenny	3,319	2	0	1		0	5	4	0
Laois	3,015	2	1	1		1	3	4	102
Tipp.Sth*	3,557	4	0	1		0	9	11	0

Waterford	2,359	1	0	0		0	5	5	0
Wexford	3,341	0	0	1		0	6	6	0
Sub-total	**19,702**	**9**	**1**	**4**		**1**	**37**	**38**	**102**
Clare	6,369	0	0	1		1	4	34	78
Cork Nth*	4,287	3	1	2		0	9	13	0
Cork Central*	3,981	1	0	1		1	5	5	42
Cork West*	4,532	3	3	3		1	8	15	80
Kerry	7,278	7	2	4		14	17	61	1,164
Limerick	5,920	2	0	1		0	9	11	0
Tipp.Nth*	3,535	5	2	3		3	8	11	134
Sub-total	**35,902**	**21**	**8**	**15**		**20**	**60**	**150**	**1,498**
TOTALS	**123,318**	**49**	**14**	**31**		**27**	**144**	**228**	**2,119**

* For administrative purposes Cork North, Central and West, and Tipp. North and South are calculated together

31/12/2004	124,583	102	37	63		68	283	664	5,351

The obligations imposed on the herd owner or person who controls the herd are contained in the Brucellosis in Cattle (General Provisions) Order 1991,[12] which provides as follows:-

> "(a) Section 3, Sub-Section 3 provides that the owner or person in charge of the herd shall present all eligible animals in the herd for the taking of such samples as may be necessary to test all such animals in the herd;
> (b) At the commencement of the test the owner or the person in charge of the animal or animals proposed to be tested shall surrender to the person taking the samples all identity

---

[12] S.I. No.114 of 1991.

cards in respect of any eligible animals and female animals aged less than 12 months;

(c) Where the person who has taken such samples has been notified by a district veterinary office that any animal concerned is given a positive reaction to the test, that person shall forward to the district veterinary office in the area in which the sample was taken, all identity cards surrendered to him in accordance with sub-paragraph (b) of this paragraph;

(d) Where the person who has taken such samples has been notified by a district veterinary office that none of the animals tested has given a positive or inconclusive reaction to the test, that person shall endorse each of the identity cards for eligible animals surrendered to him in accordance with sub-paragraph (b) of this paragraph with an indication that the animal concerned has passed the test and shall return such cards, when duly endorsed, to either the herd owner or person in charge of the herd;

(e) Where the person who takes such samples has been notified by a district veterinary office that none of the animals tested is given a positive result but that the result of the test of an animal or animals has been inconclusive the person shall –

  i.   Forward to the district veterinary office the identity card of each animal as respects which the result was inconclusive, and,

  ii. Endorse each of the remaining identity cards for eligible animals surrendered to him in accordance with sub-paragraph

    (b) of this paragraph with an indication that the animal concerned has passed the test and return those cards when duly endorsed and any other identity cards so surrendered to either the owner or person in charge of the herd;

(f) Where samples have been taken from all the eligible animals in the herd, no female animal of any age shall be moved out of the herd or off the land on which the samples are taken, except under and in accordance with the terms of a movement permit unless the tests have been completed by either the owner or the person in charge of the animals has been informed of the results of the tests."

In summary therefore the obligations of the farmer are:

- To present all animals,

- to surrender identity cards, and

- not to move any animals from the herd until test results are known.

Where, in compliance with a test, a veterinary inspector concludes that a reactor exists on the holding he *shall* declare the holding to be a restricted holding by serving on the owner a notice in the form set out in Part I of the Second Schedule to this Order.

The Department of Agriculture and Food's policy is to eliminate the final source of infection by depopulating brucellosis herds with the active infection, and to this end in 2001 a full round of blood testing for all eligible cattle was carried out in conjunction with the existing arrangement which include the monthly milk testing (the MRT) of dairy herds.

The movement of animals

All female cattle and bulls over 12 months of age being moved in or out of holdings must have passed a blood test within 30 days preceding the date of the movement.

The Department of Agriculture and Food guidelines provide that for a brucellosis breakdown a district veterinary office will commence completion of Form ER111 using all available information of eligible animals which possibly entered the herd during the specified period under review for determining compensation payment.

Form ER111 will be forwarded to the owner/holder who may be required to furnish additional information but he/she will be required to sign a declaration.

Each owner/holder will have a review period which is dependant upon the breakdown testing date of the last full herd test prior to breakdown. It is therefore critical that the holder/owner keeps records of all movements of animals into and out of his or her herd using the herd register (which they are obliged to do now since 2001) and keeping all other and any other available documentation in relation to the purchase, sale or removal or addition of animals to or from the herd. Therefore in the event of any breakdown it would be possible for the owner to furnish the required information in order to accelerate the implementation of the compensation process.

Brucellosis Compensation Schemes

1. On Farm Market Valuation Scheme
This scheme replaced the reactor grant element of the compensation regime with effect from April 2, 2002 for all reactors disclosed as a result of a test carried out on or after this date. The Department of Agriculture and Food guidelines defines market value as the equivalent price

which might reasonably have been obtained for the animal at the time of determination of compensation from a purchaser on the open market if the animal was not affected by TB or brucellosis or was not been removed as part of a depopulation under the disease eradication programme. Such determinations were to be made by suitably qualified valuers within the guidelines drawn up by the Department.

2. Income Supplement

As already referred to the income supplement continues to be payable in cases where the disease results in the removal of more than 10% of animals in a herd where depopulation is not deemed appropriate. Payment in respect of each animal removed as a reactor from a herd subject to a maximum of 100 animals qualifying for payment (please see above for the grant rates in relation to tuberculosis).

3. Brucellosis Income Supplement

Monthly rates from January 1 to December 31 the standard rate for a dairy cow and other animals is €25.39. In relation to other cows the standard rate is €38.09.

4. Depopulation Grants

As outlined above a holder or owner whose herd is depopulated either partially or totally in the interests of disease control may qualify for depopulation grants. These are paid for each animal removed in depopulation and for those reactors removed since the holding was restricted pursuant to the legislation as outlined above. The

Department of Agriculture and Food guidelines indicate that this depopulation must be agreed to at the time specified by the district veterinary office. The Department further outlines that if such agreement is not received and depopulation takes places subsequently the owner or holder is excluded from eligibility for depopulation grants on all past, present and future reactors during the restriction period. In terms of brucellosis the standard rate for the depopulation of a dairy cow/in-calf heifer, and pedigree bulls under 12 months of age is €126.97, the standard rate plus is €220.55, in relation to other cows and in-calf heifers the standard rate if €126.97, that applies also with the plus rate. In relation to other animals the standard rate is €38.09 and the standard rate plus is €76.18. These figures represent the maximum available payments in relation to a 4 month rest period following an outbreak of brucellosis and the actual brucellosis depopulation.

Johne's Disease

Johne's disease is an emerging problem in Ireland's cattle herds. It is chronically infectious and the clinical symptoms are characterised by chronic continuous or intermittent watery diarrhoea. While the animals continue to eat they gradually lose condition and finally die. This disease, tuberculosis and brucellosis, are notifiable diseases to the Department of Agriculture through the district veterinary office and the disease is regulated by the Johne's Disease Order 1955.[13]

The disease is caused by infection with mycobacterium avian. Most animals are infected in early life by ingestion of

---

[13] S.I. No. 86 of 1955.

the bacteria through milk, faecal contaminated matters, water feeds or services. Calves may also be infected before birth. Half of calves born to a cow with Johne's disease will be infected with the disease, however if the cow is clinically infected but not sick that percentage falls to 10%. Infection of adult animals is rare. It should also be noted that there is no satisfactory treatment and therefore the majority of animals showing clinical symptoms will eventually die of the disease. Animals most at risk include those who have been exposed to the bacteria under one year's of age or can be imported.[14]

---

[14] Further information is available from a veterinary surgeon and/or the Department of Agriculture at the website www.johnes.org.

CHAPTER 8

Boundaries, Wall and Fences

The purpose of this Chapter is to elucidate the main principles of law which are generally material in relation to the question of boundaries and fences. The subject includes fencing of land and fencing of property with regard to walls.

It is to be noted at the outset that the primary purpose of this chapter is to give an outline of the subject matter as there is a vast areas of law touching and concerning the subject, and recourse should be had to specific texts dealing with same.

Fences

The primary function of a fence is firstly to guard against intrusion and, secondly to ensure that animals do not stray upon a neighbour's land and further to limit liability for animals straying upon an owner's land. A further purpose and use for fencing is that it provides a visible boundary line between two properties. Such fence may, of course, consist of anything from a wall to a ditch, a bank, a hedge or a tree-line.

A fence may be comprised of any of the foregoing. Regardless of plans, measurements, descriptions of land as arable, pasture, woodland or waste, reference to present or former occupation and/or the name of any property, land, farm or field, the actual limits of the subject matter of a transaction concerning land depend upon the intentions of the parties to the transaction.

An intention is usually to be garnered from the document which has executed the land transaction and those terms are to be construed giving their most accurate meaning. So, in circumstances where the land is mis-described, plans are inaccurate or the intentions of the parties are not readily ascertainable from the document executing the conveyance and/or transaction, aid must be drawn from extrinsic evidence of the circumstances subsisting at the time. Further there are certain presumptions that exist which aid the Courts in determining the limits upon the property.

Presumption 1

There is a presumption that the owner of the fence also owns the ditch. There is a presumption that a ditch and fence belong to the owner of the land upon which the fence stands, so where a ditch divides a particular piece of land from a fence or bank it is presumed that the boundary of the land is at the edge of the ditch furthest from the fence.[1]

The reason given for this presumption is that when a man makes a ditch and a fence it is easier and more expedient for him to dig the ditch at the furthest limit of his land and to throw the soil dug out of the ditch onto his own land rather than to dig the ditch at some distance from the limit of his land and throw the soil towards his neighbour's land. The possibility of trespass in the former case being less than that in the latter. It is to be noted at this point that this presumption may not be applied where it is not know whether the ditch is artificial or natural in nature.

Obligation to fence

It is to be noted that a landowner cannot simply by reason of his owing property be under any obligation to fence his boundaries. However, this general rule, as with many general rules, has certain exceptions. There may be obligations to

---

[1]   C - *Vowles v. Miller* (1810), 3 Taunt. 137 at 138.

fence imposed by agreement between the parties. There may be an obligation to fence arising through pre-description. There may be an obligation to fence imposed by the nature of the land. There may be an obligation to fence imposed by the location or the use to which the land is to be put.

In circumstances where a landowner fails to fence his land so as to prevent animals escaping therefrom onto his neighbour's land that landowner is liable for the consequences of any damage caused by such escape which is discussed more fully in Chapter 6. It is, therefore, clear that it is in every landholder's interest to ensure adequate fencing upon his own land.

In relation to the obligation imposed on the landowner by express agreement, as we have already seen that there is no express obligation at Common Law for a landowner to erect and maintain a fence on his boundaries. However, he can bind himself in contract to make and ensure the maintenance of a fence upon his own land or upon that of his neighbour. This covenant remains a personal one and cannot be used to bind his successors in title. It is to be noted that it is only in the relationship between landlord and tenants that the burden of a covenant to make, repair and ensure the maintenance of a fence runs with the lessee's estate or interest.

Normal conveyancing practice in this circumstance is for the conveyancer to obtain an indemnity from his successor in title against loss suffered by him because of a future breach of covenant. However, this does not make the covenant directly enforceable against the new owner.[2]

Where a landowner having undertaken through a covenant to erect a boundary between two pieces of land, and he/she, in fact, breaches the obligations imposed by the covenant, may be subject to liability for the costs associated with the

---

[2]   *Austerberry v. Oldham Corporation* (1885) 29 Ch.D. 750 at 781 and 782.

construction of a boundary by his adjoining neighbour.

With regard to landlord and tenants apart from the express provisions in the lease and the statutory provisions relating to agricultural holdings, the occupier of a premises let for a term of years is liable to repair fences, but tenants from year to year or at will are not. The 1791 case of *Cheetham v. Hampson*[3] is authority for the fact that the landlord can maintain an action against a tenant where the repairs are not carried out on the grounds of damage to the landlord's inheritance. Provided the landlord has not undertaken to repair the fences and they are not dilapidated at the start of the term of the Lease, the occupier will be liable to any third party injured because of want of repair.

In the case of agricultural land, it was the usual practice as stated above to dig a ditch at the outer edge of the boundary and place the earth on the owner's as opposed to the neighbour's side of the ditch and thereupon to plant the hedgerow.

This so called *"hedge and ditch rule"* was affirmed and qualified by the House of Lords in the case of *Alan Wibberley Building Limited v. Dinstey*[4] where Lord Hoffman explained the rationale as follows:

It should be noted that this rule involves two successive presumptions. First, it was presumed that the ditch was dug after the boundary was drawn. Secondly, it was then presumed that the ditch was dug and the hedge grown in a manner described by Laurence J.[5]

> "If the first presumption is displaced by evidence
> which shows that the ditch was in existence
> before the boundary was drawn, for example, as

---

[3] [1791] 4 Tern. Rep. 318.
[4] [1999] 1 W.L.R. 894.
[5] As referred to earlier *Vowles v. Millary* (1810) Taunt. 137 at 138.

an internal draining ditch which was later used
as a boundary when part of the land was sold,
then there is obviously no room for the reasoning
of Laurence J. to operate."

If, therefore, a wall or hedge appears to be surrounding the
property of one of the parties or surrounding property of which
his land once formed part, this is an indication that the
boundary feature was part of that land. Where the feature is
a hedge and ditch it would be necessary to look at the purpose
of the ditch.

Party Walls

Part 7, chapter 3 of the Land and Conveyancing Law Reform
Bill 2006, at section 42 thereof provides as follows:

"Subject to subsection 2 a building owner may
carry out works to a party structure for the
purposes of –
(a) compliance with any statutory provision or
any notice or Order under such provision or
(b) carrying out developments, which is
exempted development or development for
which Planning Permission has been
obtained or compliance with any condition
attached to such permission or
(c) preservation of the party structure of any
building or unbuilt on land of which it forms
a part or
(d) carrying out any other works which –
    i.   will not cause substantial damage or
         inconvenience to the adjoining owner,
         or
    ii. if they may or will cause such damage

or inconvenience, it is nevertheless reasonable to carry them out."

Section 42(2) provides, subject to section 42(3):-

"In exercising any rights under Sub-Section 1 the building owner shall –

(a) make good all damage caused to the adjoining owner as a consequence of the works, or reimburse the adjoining owner the reasonable costs and expense of such making good.

(b) Pay the adjoining owner –
  (i) the reasonable costs of obtaining processional advice with regard to the likely consequences of the work,
  (ii) reasonable compensation for any inconvenience caused by the works.
  (iii) The building owner may –
    (a) claim from the adjoining owner as contribution to, or deduct from any reimbursement of, the costs and expenses of making good such damage under subsection 2 (a).
    (b) Deduct from compensation under Sub-Section 2 (b) (ii) such sum as will take into account the proportionate use or enjoyment of the party structure which the adjoining owner makes or, it is reasonable to assume is likely to make.
  (iv) If –
    (a) building owner fails within a reasonable time to –
      (i) make good damage or to

> reimburse the costs and
> expenses under subsection 2(a)
> or
> (ii) pay reasonable costs or
> compensation under Sub-
> section 2(b) the adjoining owner
> may recover such costs and
> expenses or compensation as a
> simple contract debt in a Court
> of competent jurisdiction.
> (b) An adjoining owner fails to meet a
> claim to the contribution under
> subsection 3(a) the building owner
> may recover such contribution as a
> simple contract debt in a Court of
> competent jurisdiction."

To that end the party structure within the legislation is defined
as any arch, ceiling, ditch, fence, floor, hedge, partition, shrub,
tree, wall or other structure which horizontally, vertically or
in any other way –

> (a) divides adjoining and separately owned
> buildings, or
> (b) is situated at or on or close to the boundary
> line between adjoining and separately owned
> buildings or between such building and
> unbuilt on land that it is impossible or not
> reasonably practical to carry out works to
> the structure without access to the adjoining
> building or unbuilt on land, and includes any
> structure which is –
> (i) situated entirely in or on one of the
> adjoining buildings or unbuilt land, or
> (ii) straddles the boundary line between
> adjoining buildings or between such

buildings and unbuilt on lands as is either co-owned by their respective owners or subject to some division of ownership between them.

Section 43(1) provides –

a. A building owner who is in dispute with an adjoining owner with respect to exercise of rights under section 42 may apply to the Court for an Order authorising the carrying out of specified works, otherwise known as a Works Order.

b. In determining whether to make a Works Order and if one is to be made what terms and conditions should be attached to it the Court shall have regard to section 42 and may take into account any other circumstances which it considers relevant.

The Court is given considerable discretion under section 44(1) which states:

"Subject to subsection 3 a Works Order shall authorise the carrying out of works specified on such terms and condition as the Court thinks fit in the circumstances of the case. Subsection 2 without prejudice to the generality of Sub-section 1 a Works Order may –

a. authorise the building owner and that owner's agents, employees or servants to enter on an adjoining owner's building or unbuilt on land for any purpose connection with the works.

b. Require the building owner to indemnify or give security to the adjoining owner for

        damage, cost and expense caused by or
        arising from the works or likely so to be
        caused or to arise.

    c.   A works Order shall not authorise any
        permanent interference with or loss of any
        easement of light or other easement or other
        right relating to a party structure."

Section 45 reads:-

        "On the Application of any person affected by a
        Works Order, the Court may discharge or modify
        the Order on such terms and conditions as it
        thinks fit."

This, in effect, represents the proposed new legislative code
in relation to party walls and/or party structures. However, it
is proposed at this juncture to examine the previous judicial
decisions from this jurisdiction and from that of the United
Kingdom in order to ascertain what, in fact, the legal position
in relation to party walls and party structures prior to the
enactment of his new legislation is.

    The decision of *Watson v. Gray*[6] attempts a four part
definition of party wall:-

        *"The words appear to me to express a
        meaning…and they, I think, can be used in four
        different senses. They may mean first a wall of
        which two adjoining owners or Tenants in
        Common, as in Wiltshire v. Sidford[7] and Cubitt
        v. Porter.[8] I think the Judgment in those cases
        show that that is the most common and primary*

---

6   [1880] 14 Ch.D. 192 at 194.
7   [1827] 1 MAN. and RY. 404.
8   [1828] 8 B. & C. 257.

> *meaning of the term. In the next place the term*
> *may be used to signify a wall divided*
> *longitudinally into two strips, one belonging to*
> *each of the neighbouring owners, as in Marks v.*
> *Hawkins. Thirdly, the term may mean a wall*
> *which belongs entirely to one of the adjoining*
> *owners, but is subject to an easement or right in*
> *the other to have it maintained as a dividing wall*
> *between the two Tenants. The term is so used in*
> *some of the Building Acts. Lastly, the term may*
> *designate a long dividing longitudinally into two*
> *moieties, each moiety being subject to a cross-*
> *easement in favour of the other moiety."*

It is clear from this attempt at a definition which dates back to 1880 that the above referred to Bill has, in fact, reduced the four options to the two which would encompass a situation where firstly a party wall and or any other boundary is built entirely on one of the party's lands therein. The boundary would, in fact, be legally attached to the land which exists, presumably being at its outermost borders. The second situation envisaged by the new Bill is a boundary which, in fact, sits exactly on the border which separates the two properties whether, in fact, that is co-owned or subjected to some alternative division of ownership between those two parties.

As far back as the 16th Century it was decided that if an owner built the wall straddling his boundary the adjoining owner could remove part of the wall on his land.[9] In that case the wall was a dam and when the adjoining owner removed part of it; it fell down and *"the water did run out"*. This wall was not, however, a true party wall since it had been erected by one owner for his own use. What, in fact, the wall was, was a trespassing wall. The categorisations in

---

[9]   *Wigford v. Gill* [1592] 33 CRO. ELIZ. 269.

relation to walls dividing property as it stands *now prior to the enactment of the* Bill would appear to be these three –

1. Firstly where a wall is divided vertically in half each neighbour would own the half on his side.

2. Secondly where the wall is entirely on the property of one adjoining owner but is subject to easements or rights in favour of the other to have it maintained dividing the properties.

3. Thirdly, and most often where the wall is divided vertically but each part is subject to a cross-easement in favour of the other. This would obviously avoid the situation which arose in *Wigford and Gill* as above, and the practical significance of this in reality is that each party given their adjoined status and/ or their neighbouring status is required to have due consideration at Law for the fact that where a boundary wall is said to lie on the boundary and where each party is said to own half of the same wall, then upon a vertical division of same it is not practical, feasible and/or desirable for one party to remove his or her side of the wall for whatever the reason may be.

In those circumstances it is clear that the reality of the situations dictates that where a party wall is said to straddle the border between the two properties, then the likelihood of a successful division of same would be small.

Repair of party walls:

The repair obligations relating to any party wall will often be governed, in fact, by the contract between the parties however, where a question may arise under a Lease.

In the alternative, the new Bill as outlined above at section 42(2) thereof may be required in effect to maintain and/or repair any damages caused during the course of works to any party structure.

Increase in the height of a party wall owned in common:

> *"Hunt on Boundaries"*, the 6th Edition dated 1912 at page 132 thereof provides as follows:-
>> *"Where the Plaintiff and Defendant were respective owners of adjoining house, and at the rear of each house there was a yard and the two yards were separate by a wall, and it appeared that the Plaintiff, in the course of erecting a shed in his backyard adjoined to the separation wall, built on the top of that wall without the Defendant's permission a new piece of wall of a triangular shape, and the Defendant knocked down this new piece of wall, the Court was of the opinion that the Defendant was justified in doing what he had done."*

This is cited from the Judgment of *Watson v. Gray*.[10]

Distinction between a boundary wall and a party wall

The question has arisen as to whether or not a boundary wall or other structure is, in fact, a party wall in the strict sense. The answer to this question is usually dependent upon the

---

[10] [1880] 14 Ch.D. 192.

terms of any conveyance or other disposition implication by Statute or the outcome of any dispute resolution which is envisaged under the new Bill and, of course, as already outlined at the beginning of this Chapter by implication of the presumed intention of the parties. It has become common practice that the conveyance or disposition will often provide specifically that a particular wall shall be a party wall or a boundary wall or that all boundary walls shall, in fact, be party walls. This is more often the case in urbanized area where large housing estates are involved.

Common law obligations

An easement for support of one part of a party wall by another in separate ownership may be acquired by grant, express or implied, or by prescription as outlined above. In the absence of acquisition by any of these methods there is no right of support as per *Peyton v. London Corporation.*[11] However, in situations where the support is, in fact, wrongfully withdrawn there will lie in Law an action for nuisance and even where damage has been suffered the adjoining owner is not liable for merely failing to keep his building or part of the wall in repair, but will be liable only for positive acts resulting in the withdrawal of support.[12]

In relation to repairs, an easement of support does not cast upon the joint owner of the party wall any positive obligation to keep his part of the wall in repair. Similar duties may nevertheless arise as a result of the Law on nuisance. Again *Sack v. Jones* is authority for the fact that if a party wall collapses because of the neglect by one owner the other owner has, in fact, no right of action. However, the other owner may not needlessly sit by and watch the wall fall into

---

[11] [1829] 9 B. & C. 725.
[12] *Sack v. Jones* [1925] Ch. 235.

disrepair and disintegrate and may, in fact, enter his
neighbour's property in order to carry out repairs. This
position of the Law is, in fact, reflected in section 42 (1) (c)
of the Land Reform and Conveyancing Bill 2006, wherein
*"a building owner may carry out works to a party structure
for the purposes of the preservation of the party structure or
of any building or unbuilt on land of which it forms a part."*
This again would seem to reflect the Common Law position
which existed and continues to exist up to the enactment of
the legislation which is envisaged to happen subsequent to
the publication of this work.

The judgment of Lavery J. of the High Court in *Patrick
Winters v. Owens*[13] provides at page 228 thereof:-

> *"There is no doubt as to the legal position
> between adjoining owners of land. A landowner
> is under no legal obligation apart from special
> classes of customer contract to fence his land so
> as to prevent the entry thereon of trespassing
> animals. A landowner is bound by Law to fence
> his land so as to prevent animals escaping
> therefrom and trespassing on adjoining lands,
> and he is liable for damage done to his
> neighbour's land and crops if he fails in this
> duty."*

Useful guidance in the case of *Persian Properties Limited
and the Registrar of Titles and the Minister for Finance,*
which is a judgment of the Supreme Court delivered on
February 20, 2003 by The Chief Justice Keane. He stated as
follows:-

> *"The Local Registration of Title (Ireland) Act,
> 1891"*, which was replaced by the Registration

---

[13] [1950] I.R. 225.

of Title Act 1964 *"was intended to provide in
Ireland the system of registration of title which
would relieve the owners of registered land from
the difficulties of establishing their title to land
which were the lot of owners of unregistered land
throughout the then United Kingdom and which
were associated with the notorious complexity
of the English Law of real property. Those
landowners were always exposed to the risk of
having the documentary title to their land
impugned because of frailties in the chain of title
stretching back, it might well be, to root of title
in the distant past. Save in cases of "actual fraud
or mistake", the owners of registered land were
in the far more advantageous position of being
entitled to rely on the Register, and the Register
alone, as conclusive evidence of their title "as
appearing on the Register. But since it was also
obvious that, in any such system, errors would
occur in the actual delineation of the boundaries
and the extent of the land in question, Section
85 went on to provide that the description of the
land in the Registry was not to be conclusive as
the "boundaries or extent" of the lands."*

Trees

Mills v. Brooker[14] on appeal to the Court of Kings Bench in
relation to the appropriation of apples from an overhanging
branch where the branch spanned the boundary between the
two properties, pursuant to the decision in *Lemmon v. Webb*[15]
where the Court held that the neighbour was entitled without
notice if he did not trespass on his neighbour's land to cut

[14] [1919] 1 KB.555.
[15] [1894] 4 Ch. 1.

the branches of an overhanging tree, which hung over his boundary so far as they overhung although they had, in fact, done so for 20 years. A Court of Appeal in the House of Lords held that an aggrieved party cannot go on to the soil of a neighbour to remove a nuisance unless he first gives his neighbour notice to remove it. Pursuant to that decision in *Mills v. Brooker* the Court of Appeal held –

> "The owner of a fruit tree the branch of which grows over the boundary of his land is the owner of the fruit on the overhanging branch while it is still growing on the tree. The adjoining owner is entitled to sever the branch but that does not divest the owner's right of property. The adjoining owner is not entitled to sell the fruit."

As outlined above party structure is defined in the Land and Conveyancing Law Reform Bill 2006, as:-

> "Any arch, ceiling, ditch, fence, floor, hedge, partition, shrub, tree, wall or other structure which horizontally, vertically and divides adjoining or separately owned properties."

Therefore, it is envisioned within the new Legislative code that the same legal requirements attached to the damage caused to trees as it would be to boundary walls. However, again reference is drawn to the above quoted section 42 of the Land and Conveyancing Law Reform Bill of 2006 that:

> *"a building owner may carry out works to a party structure for the purposes of compliance with statutory provision, carrying out exempted development, carrying out development for which planning permission had been obtained, the preservation of a party structure and finally*

> *carrying out other works which will not cause*
> *substantial damage or inconvenience to the*
> *adjoining owner."*

General rules as to the ownership of boundary trees

The ownership of a tree which stands or grows on the boundary of properties between two adjoining owners depends upon the question of who planted or sowed that tree. The tree belongs to the owner in whose ground the tree was first sown or planted. It should be noted, indeed, at this point that the spread of roots onto adjoining property subsequent to the planning of the tree will not entitle the owner of the adjoining property to subsequent ownership of the tree. As per the cases of *Masters v. Pollie*[16] *and Lemmon v. Webb*,[17] it was provided in relation to the former that where the identity of the planter of the tree is not available, it will depend upon the geographical situation of the tree, and in relation to the latter case, if a tree is situate exactly equally between the properties and in the absence of any ownership claims by either party, the tree will be presumed to both adjoining owners as Tenants in Common.

Remedies available

The remedies available for injuries arising from overhanging branches or projecting roots are generally to be found in the Tort of Nuisance. The remedies available are an action for damages caused for the loss, secondly a Mandatory Injunction for the removal of the offending article and thirdly, the landowner may himself abate the nuisance by removal of so much of the branches as overhang his land. As stated already

---

[16] [1620] 2 ROLLE, 141.
[17] [1894] 3 Ch. 1 at 20.

in *Lemmon v. Webb* a landowner may cut the branches of his neighbour's tree where those branches overhang the owner's land. It would appear that he does not have to show that it was likely the overhanging braches would have caused damage. However that case further provides that a landowner may not cut the branches of a tree if he is doing so merely in anticipation of the offending branches crossing the boundaries.

In relation to roots the problems which arise are often more serious given the damages that roots may cause to property. Further as with all things natural it is very difficult for any party to control the growth of the roots of trees once factors such as the species of tree, the age of the tree, the nature and depth of the soil, its moisture content and proximity to other trees and other impingements in the soil. In *Middleton v. Humphreys*,[18] the plaintiff complained that the boundary wall which separated his property from his neighbours had been damaged by the growth of roots of trees in the ownership of the neighbour. In that case Mr. Justice Ross examined the factual circumstances in relation to the probable causes of any damage which was, in fact, caused. In that Judgment he put great weight on the power of growing roots on walls stating that "*it is unwise to have trees near walls*". In that instance the Judge awarded a Declaration that the defendant had wrongfully permitted the roots of trees to grow under the plaintiff's wall. He also granted an Injunction restraining the defendant from continuing to permit such injury to accrue.

Subsequent English and Irish judgments support this position and the actions are usually maintained on the basis of the fact that the encroachment of roots onto a neighbour's land is not a trespass, it is a nuisance and, therefore, an action lies in damages and a neighbour may, in fact, abate the nuisance if the owner of the tree, after having been given notice, fails, in fact, to abate such nuisance.

---

[18] [1913] 47 I.L.T.R. 160.

APPENDIX 1

S.I. No. 378 of 2006

European Communities (Good Agricultural Practice for Protection of Waters) Regulations 2006

PART 1
PRELIMINARY

PART 2
FARMYARD MANAGEMENT

PART 3
NUTRIENT MANAGEMENT

PART 4
PREVENTION OF WATER POLLUTION FROM FERTILISERS AND CERTAIN ACTIVITIES

PART 5
GENERAL

PART 6
FUNCTIONS OF PUBLIC AUTHORITIES

SCHEDULES

S.I. No. 378 of 2006

European Communities (Good Agricultural Practice for Protection of Waters) Regulations 2006

The Minister for the Environment, Heritage and Local Government in exercise of the powers conferred on him by section 3 of the European Communities Act 1972 (No. 27 of 1972) and for the purposes of giving further effect to Directive 75/442/EEC of 15 July 1975,[1] Directive 76/464/EEC of 4 May 1976,[2] Directive 80/68/EEC of 17 December 1979,[3] Directive 91/676/EEC of 12 December 1991,[4] Directive 2000/60/EC of 23 October 2000[5] and Directive 2003/35/EC of 26 May 2003[6] hereby makes the following Regulations:

PART 1
PRELIMINARY

Citation and commencement

1.   (a)   These Regulations may be cited as the European Communities (Good Agricultural Practice for Protection of Waters) Regulations 2006.

     (b)   These Regulations shall come into effect on 1 August, 2006 save as is otherwise provided in relation to any particular provision.

Revocations

2. The European Communities (Protection of Waters Against Pollution from Agricultural Sources) Regulations, 2003 (S.I. No.213 of 2003) and the European Communities (Good Agricultural Practice for Protection of Waters) Regulations, 2005 (S.I. No. 788 of 2005) are hereby revoked.

---

1.   O.J. No. L 194/39, 25 July 1975.
2.   O.J. No. L 129/23, 18 May 1976.
3.   O.J. No. L 20/43, 26 January 1980.
4.   O.J. No L 375/1, 31 December 1991.
5.   O.J. No. L 327/1, 22 December 2000.
6.   O.J. No. L 156/17, 25 June 2003.

Interpretation

3. (1) In these Regulations, save where the context otherwise requires–

> "Act of 1992" means the Environmental Protection Agency Act 1992 (No. 7 of 1992);

> "Agency" means the Environmental Protection Agency established under section 19 of the Act of 1992;

> "agriculture" includes the breeding, keeping and sale of livestock (including cattle, horses, pigs, poultry, sheep and any creature kept for the production of food, wool, skins or fur), the making and storage of silage, the cultivation of land, and the growing of crops (including forestry and horticultural crops);

> "application to land", in relation to fertiliser, means the addition of fertiliser to land whether by spreading on the surface of the land, injection into the land, placing below the surface of the land or mixing with the surface layers of the land but does not include the direct deposition of manure to land by animals;

> "aquifer" means any stratum or combination of strata that stores or transmits groundwater;

> "chemical fertiliser" means any fertiliser that is manufactured by an industrial process;

> "farmyard manure" means a mixture of bedding material and animal excreta in solid form arising from the housing of cattle, sheep and other livestock excluding poultry;

> "fertiliser" means any substance containing nitrogen or phosphorus or a nitrogen compound or phosphorus compound utilised on land to enhance growth of vegetation and may include livestock manure, the residues from fish farms and sewage sludge;

> "groundwater" means all water that is below the surface of the ground in the saturation zone and in direct contact with the ground or subsoil;

> "holding" means an agricultural production unit and, in relation to an occupier, means all the agricultural production units managed by that occupier;

> "livestock" means all animals kept for use or profit (including cattle, horses, pigs, poultry, sheep and any creature kept for the production of food, wool, skins or fur);

> "livestock manure" means waste products excreted by livestock or a mixture of litter and waste products excreted by livestock, even in processed form;

"local authority" means a city council or county council within the meaning of the Local Government Act 2001 (No. 37 of 2001);

"the Minister" means the Minister for the Environment, Heritage and Local Government;

"net area", in relation to a holding and the grassland stocking rate, means the gross area of the holding or the grassland as appropriate excluding areas under farm roads, paths, buildings, farmyards, woods, dense scrub, rivers, streams, ponds, lakes, sandpits, quarries, expanses of bare rock, areas of bogland not grazed, areas fenced off and not used for production, inaccessible areas and areas of forestry (including Christmas trees), or required to be totally destocked under a Commonage Framework Plan;

"the Nitrates Directive" means Council Directive 91/676/EEC of 12 December 1991 concerning the protection of waters against pollution caused by nitrates from agricultural sources;

"occupier", in relation to a holding, includes the owner, a lessee, any person entitled to occupy the holding or any other person having for the time being control of the holding;

"organic fertiliser" means any fertiliser other than that manufactured by an industrial process and includes livestock manure, dungstead manure, farmyard manure, slurry, soiled water, non-farm organic substances such as sewage sludge, industrial by-products and sludges and residues from fish farms;

"ploughing" includes ploughing and primary cultivation, excluding light cultivation carried out to encourage natural regeneration;

"relevant local authority" means the local authority in whose administrative area a farm holding or part of a farm holding is situated;

"river basin district" means a river basin district established by the European Communities (Water Policy) Regulations, 2003 (S.I. No. 722 of 2003);

"slurry" includes –
(a) excreta produced by livestock while in a building or yard, and
(b) a mixture of such excreta with rainwater, washings or other extraneous material or any combination of these,
of a consistency that allows it to be pumped or discharged by gravity at any stage in the handling process but does not include soiled water;

"soil test" means a soil sample taken in accordance with the soil sampling procedure set out in Schedule 1 and analysed in accordance with that Schedule, at a laboratory approved for this purpose by the Minister for Agriculture and Food;

"soiled water" has the meaning assigned by sub-article (2);

"steep slope" means ground which has an average incline of 20% or more in the case of grassland or 15% or more in the case of other land;

"tidal waters" includes the sea and any estuary up to high water mark medium tide and any enclosed dock adjoining tidal waters;

"waters" includes –
(a) any (or any part of any) river, stream, lake, canal, reservoir, aquifer, pond, watercourse, or other inland waters, whether natural or artificial,
(b) any tidal waters, and
(c) where the context permits, any beach, river bank and salt marsh or other area which is contiguous to anything mentioned in paragraph (a) or (b), and the channel or bed of anything mentioned in paragraph (a) which is for the time being dry,
but does not include a sewer,

"waterlogged ground" means ground that is saturated with water such that any further addition will lead, or is likely to lead, to surface run-off;

and cognate words shall be construed accordingly.

(2)   (a)   In these Regulations "soiled water" includes, subject to this sub-article, water from concreted areas, hard standing areas, holding areas for livestock and other farmyard areas where such water is contaminated by contact with any of the following substances–
(i)   livestock faeces or urine or silage effluent,
(ii)   chemical fertilisers,
(iii)   washings such as vegetable washings, milking parlour washings or washings from mushroom houses,
(iv)   water used in washing farm equipment.
(b)   In these Regulations, "soiled water" does not include any liquid where such liquid has either –
(i)   a biochemical oxygen demand exceeding 2,500 mg per litre, or
(ii)   a dry matter content exceeding 1%.
(c)   For the purposes of these Regulations, soiled water which is stored together with slurry or which becomes mixed with slurry is deemed to be slurry.

(3) In these Regulations a reference to:-

  (a) an Article, Part or Schedule which is not otherwise identified
       is a reference to an Article, Part or Schedule of these
       Regulations,

  (b) a sub-article or paragraph which is not otherwise identified
       is a reference to a sub-article or paragraph of the provision
       in which the reference occurs, and

  (c) a period between a specified day in a month and a specified
       day in another month means the period commencing on the
       first-mentioned day in any year and ending on the second-
       mentioned day which first occurs after the first-mentioned
       day.

(4) In these Regulations a footnote to a table in Schedule 2 shall be deemed to
form part of the table.

PART 2

FARMYARD MANAGEMENT

Minimisation of soiled water

4. (1) An occupier of a holding shall take all such reasonable steps as are necessary
for the purposes of minimising the amount of soiled water produced on the holding.

   (2) Without prejudice to the generality of sub-article (1), an occupier of a
holding shall take all such reasonable steps as are necessary to ensure that rainwater
from roofs and unsoiled paved areas and water flowing from higher ground onto
a farmyard

  (a) is diverted to a clean water outfall, and

  (b) is prevented from entering onto soiled paved areas or
       otherwise becoming soiled.

(3) This article shall come into operation on 1 January 2007.

Collection and holding of certain substances

5. Livestock manure and other organic fertilisers, soiled water and effluents from
dungsteads, farmyard manure pits or silage pits arising or produced in a building
or yard on a holding shall, prior to its application to land or other treatment, be
collected and held in a manner that prevents the run-off or seepage, directly or
indirectly, into groundwaters or surface waters of such substances.

Structural integrity of storage facilities

6. (1) Storage facilities for livestock manure and other organic fertilisers, soiled water and effluents from dungsteads, farmyard manure pits or silage pits shall be maintained free of structural defect and be of such standard as is necessary to prevent run-off or seepage, directly or indirectly, into groundwater or surface water, of such substances.

(2) Storage facilities being provided on a holding on or after 1 August 2006 shall–

  (a)   be designed, sited, constructed, maintained and managed so as to prevent run-off or seepage, directly or indirectly, into groundwater or surface water of a substance specified in sub-article (1), and

  (b)   comply with such construction specifications for those facilities as may be approved from time to time by the Minister for Agriculture and Food.

(3) In this article "storage facilities" includes out-wintering pads, earthen-lined stores, integrated constructed wetlands and any other system used for the holding or treatment of livestock manure or other organic fertilisers.

General obligations as to capacity of storage facilities

7. (1) The capacity of storage facilities for livestock manure and other organic fertilisers, soiled water and effluents from dungsteads, farmyard manure pits or silage pits on a holding shall be adequate to provide for the storage of all such substances as are likely to require storage on the holding for such period as may be necessary as to ensure compliance with these Regulations and the avoidance of water pollution.

(2) For the purposes of sub-article (1) an occupier shall have due regard to the storage capacity likely to be required during periods of adverse weather conditions when, due to extended periods of wet weather, frozen ground or otherwise, the application to land of livestock manure or soiled water is precluded.

(3) For the purposes of Articles 7 to 13, the capacity of storage facilities on a holding shall be disregarded insofar as the occupier does not have exclusive use of those facilities.

(4) For the purposes of Articles 9 to 13 the capacity of facilities required in accordance with these Regulations for the storage of manure from livestock of the type specified in Tables 1, 2 or 3 of Schedule 2 shall be determined by reference to the criteria set out in the relevant table and the rainfall criteria set out in Table 4 of that schedule and shall include capacity for the storage for such period as may be necessary for compliance with these Regulations of rainwater, soiled water or other extraneous water which enters or is likely to enter the facilities.

Capacity of storage facilities for effluents and soiled water

8. Without prejudice to the generality of Article 7, the capacity of facilities for the storage on a holding of–

      (a)   effluent produced by ensiled forage and other crops shall equal or exceed the capacity specified in Table 5 of Schedule 2, and

      (b)   soiled water shall equal or exceed the capacity required to store all soiled water likely to arise on the holding during a period of 10 days.

Capacity of storage facilities for pig manure

9. (1) Without prejudice to the generality of Article 7, the capacity of facilities for the storage on a holding of livestock manure produced by pigs shall, subject to sub-article (2) and Article 13, equal or exceed the capacity required to store all such livestock manure produced on the holding during a period of 26 weeks.

    (2) The period specified in Schedule 3 shall, in substitution for that prescribed by sub-article (1), apply in relation to livestock manure produced by pigs on a holding in case where all the following conditions are met –

      (a)   the number of pigs on the holding does not at any time exceed one hundred pigs, and

      (b)   the holding comprises a sufficient area of land for the application in accordance with these Regulations of all livestock manure produced on the holding.

Capacity of storage facilities for poultry manure

10. (1) Without prejudice to the generality of Article 7, the capacity of facilities for the storage on a holding of livestock manure produced by poultry shall, subject to sub-article (2) and Article 13, equal or exceed the capacity required to store all such livestock manure produced on the holding during a period of 26 weeks.

    (2) The period specified in Schedule 3 shall, in substitution for that prescribed by sub-article (1), apply in relation to livestock manure produced by poultry on a holding in case where all the following conditions are met –

      (a)   tillage or grassland farming is carried out on the holding,

      (b)   the number of poultry places on the holding does not exceed 2,000 places, and

      (c)   the holding comprises a sufficient area of land for the application in accordance with these Regulations of all livestock manure produced on the holding.

Capacity of storage facilities for manure from deer, goats and sheep

11. Without prejudice to the generality of Article 7, the capacity of facilities for the storage on a holding of livestock manure produced by deer, goats and sheep shall, subject to Article 13, equal or exceed the capacity required to store all such livestock manure produced on the holding during a period of six weeks.

Capacity of storage facilities for manure from cattle

12. Without prejudice to the generality of Article 7, the capacity of facilities for the storage on a holding of livestock manure produced by cattle shall, subject to Article 13, equal or exceed the capacity required to store all such livestock manure produced on the holding during the period specified in Schedule 3.

Reduced storage capacity in certain circumstances

13. (1) The capacity of facilities for the storage of livestock manure on a holding may, to such extent as is justified in the particular circumstances of the holding, be less than the capacity specified in Article 9, 10, 11 or 12, as appropriate, in the case of a holding where –

  (a)   the occupier of the holding has a contract providing exclusive access to adequate alternative storage capacity located outside the holding,

  (b)   the occupier has a contract for access to a treatment facility for livestock manure, or

  (c)   the occupier has a contract for the transfer of the manure to a person authorised under and in accordance with the Waste Management Acts 1996 to 2003 or the Environmental Protection Agency Acts 1992 and 2003 to undertake the collection, recovery or disposal of the manure.

(2) Subject to sub-article (3), the capacity of facilities for the storage of livestock manure may be less than the capacity specified in Article 11 or 12, as appropriate, in relation to –

  (a)   deer, goats or sheep which are out-wintered at a grassland stocking rate which does not exceed 130 kg nitrogen at any time during the period specified in Schedule 4 in relation to the application of organic fertiliser other than farmyard manure, or

  (b)   livestock (other than dairy cows, deer, goats or sheep) which are out-wintered at a grassland stocking rate which does not exceed 85 kg nitrogen at any time during the period specified in Schedule 4 in relation to the application of organic fertiliser other than farmyard manure.

(3) Sub-article (2) shall apply only in relation to a holding where all the following conditions are met–

> (a) all the lands used for out-wintering of the livestock are comprised in the holding,
> (b) the out-wintered livestock have free access at all times to the required lands,
> (c) the amount of manure produced on the holding does not exceed an amount containing 140kg of nitrogen per hectare per annum,
> (d) severe damage to the surface of the land by poaching does not occur, and
> (e) the reduction in storage capacity is proportionate to the extent of out-wintered livestock on the holding.

(4) In this article, a grassland stocking rate of 130 kg or 85kg of nitrogen, as the case may be, means the stocking of grassland on a holding at any time by such numbers and types of livestock as would in the course of a year excrete waste products containing 130 kg or 85 kg of nitrogen, as the case may be, per hectare of the grassland when calculated in accordance with the nutrient excretion rates for livestock specified in Table 6 of Schedule 2.

Operative dates

14. (1) In the case of a holding on which there are in place on 1 August 2006 storage facilities in compliance with the storage capacity requirements prescribed by Articles 8, 9, 10, 11 or 12, the relevant article and Article 7 shall come into effect in relation to those facilities on 1 August 2006.

(2) In the case of a holding on which there are not in place on 1 August 2006 storage facilities in compliance with the storage capacity requirements prescribed by Article 9, that article and Article 7 shall come into effect in relation to those facilities on 31 December 2006 or the day on which such storage facilities are put in place on that holding, whichever day first occurs.

(3) In the case of a holding on which there are not in place on 1 August 2006 storage facilities in compliance with the storage capacity requirements prescribed by Article 8, 10, 11 or 12, the relevant article and Article 7 shall come into effect on 31 December 2008 or the day on which such storage facilities are put in place on that holding, whichever day first occurs.

(4) Save as is otherwise provided by this article, Article 7 shall come into operation on 31 December 2008.

PART 3
Nutrient Management

Interpretation, commencement etc

15. (1) In this Part, "crop requirement", in relation to the application of fertilisers to promote the growth of a crop, means the amounts and types of fertilisers which are reasonable to apply to soil for the purposes of promoting the growth of the crop having regard to the foreseeable nutrient supply available to the crop from the fertilisers, the soil and from other sources.

(2) The amount of nitrogen or phosphorus specified in Table 7 or 8 of Schedule 2, as the case may be, in relation to a type of livestock manure or other substance specified in the relevant table shall for the purposes of this Part be deemed to be the amount of nitrogen or phosphorus, as the case may be, contained in that type of manure or substance except as may be otherwise specified in a certificate issued in accordance with Article 32.

(3) The amount of nitrogen or phosphorus available to a crop from a fertiliser of a type which is specified in Table 9 of Schedule 2 in the year of application of that fertiliser shall, for the purposes of this Part, be deemed to be the percentage specified in that table of the amount of nitrogen or phosphorus, as the case may be, in the fertiliser.

(4) The amount of nitrogen or phosphorus available to a crop from an organic fertiliser of a type which is not specified in Table 9 of Schedule 2 shall be deemed to be the amount specified in that table in relation to cattle manure unless a different amount has been determined in relation to that fertiliser by, or with the agreement of, the relevant local authority or the Agency, as the case may be.

(5) A reference in this Part to the "nitrogen index" or the "phosphorus index" in relation to soil is a reference to the index number assigned to the soil in accordance with Table 10 or 11 of Schedule 2, as the case may be, to indicate the level of nitrogen or phosphorus available from the soil.

(6) This Part shall come into operation on 1 January 2007.

Duty of occupier in relation to nutrient management

16. (1) An occupier of a holding shall take all such reasonable steps as are necessary for the purposes of preventing or minimising the application to land of fertilisers in excess of crop requirement on the holding.

(2)   (a)   For the purposes of this article the phosphorus index for soil shall be deemed to be phosphorus index 3 unless a soil test indicates that a different phosphorus index is appropriate in relation to that soil.

         (b)   The soil test to be taken into account for the purposes of paragraph (a) in relation to soil shall, subject to paragraph (c), be the soil test most recently taken in relation to that soil.

(c)   Where a period of six years or more has elapsed after the
taking of a soil test in relation to soil the results of that test
shall be disregarded for the purposes of paragraph (a) except
in a case where that soil test indicates the soil to be at
phosphorus index 4.

(3) Without prejudice to the generality of sub-article (1) and subject to sub-article
(4), the amount of available nitrogen or available phosphorus applied to promote
the growth of a crop specified in Table 12, 13, 14, 15, 16, 17, 18, 19, 20 or 21 of
Schedule 2 shall not exceed the amount specified in the table in relation to that
crop having regard to the relevant nitrogen index or phosphorus index, as the case
may be, for the soil on which the crops are to be grown.

(4) In the case of a holding on which grazing livestock are held, the amount
of available phosphorus supplied to the holding by the concentrated feedstuff fed
to such livestock shall be deemed to be 0.5 kg phosphorus in respect of each 100
kg of such concentrated feedstuff.

(5)   (a)   In the case of a holding on which grazing livestock are held,
the amount of available nitrogen and available phosphorus
supplied to the holding by manure from such livestock shall
(save insofar as such manure is exported from the holding)
be deemed to be the relevant proportion of the amount of
available nitrogen and available phosphorus contained in
the total manure produced by such livestock.
(b)   In paragraph (a), the "relevant proportion" means the
proportion of a year as is represented by the storage period
specified in Schedule 3 in relation to the holding.

PART 4
PREVENTION OF WATER POLLUTION FROM FERTILISERS AND CERTAIN ACTIVITIES

Distances from a water body and other issues

17. (1) Chemical fertiliser shall not be applied to land within 1.5 metres of a
surface watercourse.

(2) Organic fertiliser or soiled water shall not be applied to land within –

(a)   subject to sub-article (5), 200m of the abstraction point of
any surface watercourse, borehole, spring or well used for
the abstraction of water for human consumption in a water
scheme supplying 100m^3 or more of water per day or serving
500 or more persons,
(b)   subject to sub-article (5), 100m of the abstraction point
(other than an abstraction point specified at paragraph (a))

of any surface watercourse, borehole, spring or well used for the abstraction of water for human consumption in a water scheme supplying 10m³ or more of water per day or serving 50 or more persons,

(c)   subject to sub-article (5), 25m of any borehole, spring or well used for the abstraction of water for human consumption other than a borehole, spring or well specified at paragraph (a) or (b),

(d)   20m of a lake shoreline,

(e)   15m of exposed cavernous or karstified limestone features (such as swallow-holes and collapse features), or

(f)   subject to sub-articles (8) and (9), 5m of a surface watercourse (other than a lake or a surface watercourse specified at paragraph (a) or (b)).

(3) Where farmyard manure is held in a field prior to landspreading it shall be held in a compact heap and shall not be placed within–

(a)   250m of the abstraction point of any surface watercourse or borehole, spring or well used for the abstraction of water for human consumption in a water scheme supplying 10m³ or more of water per day or serving 50 or more persons,

(b)   50m of any other borehole, spring or well used for the abstraction of water for human consumption other than a borehole, spring or well specified at paragraph (a),

(c)   20m of a lake shoreline,

(d)   50m of exposed cavernous or karstified limestone features (such as swallow-holes and collapse features),

(e)   10m of a surface watercourse (other than a lake or a surface watercourse specified at paragraph (a)).

(4) Farmyard manure shall not be held in a field at any time during the periods specified in Schedule 4 as applicable to that substance.

(5)   (a)   A local authority may, in the case of any particular abstraction point and following consultation with the Agency, specify an alternative distance to that specified in sub-article (2)(a), (b) or (c) where, following prior investigations, the authority is satisfied that such other distance as may be specified by the authority is appropriate for the protection of waters being abstracted at that point.

(b)   A distance specified by a local authority in accordance with paragraph (a) may be described as a distance or distances from an abstraction point, a geological or other topographical feature or as an area delineated on a map or in such other way as appears appropriate to the authority.

(6) In sub-article (5), "prior investigations" means, in relation to an abstraction point, an assessment of the susceptibility of waters to contamination in the vicinity of the abstraction point having regard to–

(a) the direction of flow of surface water or groundwater, as the case may be,
(b) the slope of the land,
(c) the natural geological and hydrogeological attributes of the area including the nature and depth of any overlying soil and subsoil and its effectiveness in preventing or reducing the entry of harmful substances to water, and
(d) where relevant, the technical specifications set out in the document "Groundwater Protection Schemes" (and the relevant groundwater protection responses) published in 1999 (ISBN 1-899702-22-9) or any subsequent published amendment of that document.

(7) Where a local authority specifies an alternative distance in accordance with sub-article (5) the authority shall, as soon as may be –

(a) notify the affected landowners and the Department of Agriculture and Food of the distance so specified,
(b) send to the Agency a summary of the report on the prior investigations carried for the purpose and the reasons for specifying the alternative distance, and
(c) make an entry in the register maintained in accordance with Article 30(6).

(8) The distance of 5m specified in sub-article (2)(f) may be reduced to 3m where one of the following conditions is met -

(a) the watercourse is an open drain, or
(b) the area of land adjacent to the watercourse is a narrow parcel of land not exceeding one hectare in area and not more than 50m in width.

(9) Notwithstanding sub-articles (2)(f) and (8), organic fertiliser or soiled water shall not be applied to land within 10m of a surface watercourse where the land has an average incline greater than 10% towards the watercourse.

Requirements as to manner of application of fertilisers, soiled water etc

18. (1) Livestock manure and other organic fertilisers, effluents and soiled water shall be applied to land in as accurate and uniform a manner as is practically possible.

(2) Fertilisers or soiled water shall not be applied to land in any of the following circumstances –

    (a)   the land is waterlogged;

    (b)   the land is flooded or likely to flood;

    (c)   the land is snow-covered or frozen;

    (d)   heavy rain is forecast within 48 hours, or

    (e)   the ground slopes steeply and, taking into account factors such as proximity to waters, soil condition, ground cover and rainfall, there is significant risk of causing water pollution.

(3) A person shall, for the purposes of sub-article (2)(d), have regard to weather forecasts issued by Met Éireann.

    (4) Organic fertilisers or soiled water shall not be applied to land -

    (a)   by use of an umbilical system with an upward-facing splashplate,

    (b)   by use of a tanker with an upward-facing splashplate,

    (c)   by use of a sludge irrigator mounted on a tanker, or

    (d)   from a road or passageway adjacent to the land irrespective of whether or not the road or passageway is within or outside the curtilage of the holding.

(5) Subject to sub-article (6), soiled water shall not be applied to land –

    (a)   in quantities which exceed in any period of 42 days a total quantity of 50,000 litres per hectare, or

    (b)   by irrigation at a rate exceeding 5 mm per hour.

(6) In an area which is identified on maps compiled by the Geological Survey of Ireland as "Extreme Vulnerability Areas on Karst Limestone Aquifers", soiled water shall not be applied to land –

    (a)   in quantities which exceed in any period of 42 days a total quantity of 25,000 litres per hectare, or

    (b)   by irrigation at a rate exceeding 3 mm per hour

unless the land has a consistent minimum thickness of 1m of soil and subsoil combined.

(7) For the purposes of sub-article (6), it shall be assumed until the contrary is shown that areas so identified as "Extreme Vulnerability Areas on Karst Limestone Aquifers" do not have a consistent minimum thickness of 1m of soil and subsoil combined.

Periods when application of fertilisers is prohibited

19. (1) Subject to this article, the application of fertiliser to land is prohibited during the periods specified in Schedule 4.

(2) Sub-article (1) shall come into effect on 1 August 2006 in relation to the application to land of a chemical fertiliser.

(3) Sub-article (1) shall come into effect on 1 August 2006 in relation to the application to land of organic fertiliser –

(a)   which did not arise on the holding, or

(b)   which arose on the holding in the case of a holding on which there is in place on 1 August 2006 storage facilities in compliance with the storage capacity requirements prescribed by Articles 8 to 13.

(4) In the case of a holding on which there is not in place on 1 August 2006 storage facilities in compliance with the storage capacity requirements prescribed by Articles 8 to 13, sub-article (1) shall, subject to sub-article (5), come into effect in relation to the application to land of organic fertiliser –

(a)   in the case of a pig production holding, on 31 December 2006 or the day on which such storage facilities are put in place on that holding, whichever day first occurs, and

(b)   in the case of any other holding, on 31 December 2008 or the day on which such storage facilities are put in place on that holding whichever day first occurs.

(5) Notwithstanding sub-article (4), the application of organic fertiliser to land during the months of November and December is prohibited with effect from 1 August 2006.

(6) Sub-articles (1) and (5) shall not apply in relation to the application to land of–

(a)   soiled water, or

(b)   chemical fertilisers to meet the crop requirements of Autumn-planted cabbage or of crops grown under permanent cover.

Limits on the amount of livestock manure to be applied

20. (1) Subject to this article, the amount of livestock manure applied in any year to land on a holding, together with that deposited to land by livestock, shall not exceed an amount containing 170 kg of nitrogen per hectare.

(2) For the purposes of sub-article (1), the amount of nitrogen produced by livestock and the nitrogen content of livestock manure shall be calculated in

accordance with Tables 6, 7 and 8 of Schedule 2 except in the case of pig manure or poultry manure where a different amount is specified in a certificate issued in accordance with Article 32 in relation to that manure.

(3) For the purposes of sub-article (1), the area of a holding shall be deemed to be the net area of the holding.

Ploughing and the use of non-selective herbicides

21. (1) Where arable land is ploughed between 1 July and 15 January the necessary measures shall be taken to provide for emergence, within 6 weeks of the ploughing, of green cover from a sown crop.

(2) Where grassland is ploughed between 1 July and 15 October the necessary measures shall be taken to provide for emergence by 1 November of green cover from a sown crop.

(3) Grassland shall not be ploughed between 16 October and 30 November.

(4) When a non-selective herbicide is applied to arable land or to grassland in the period between 1 July and 15 January the necessary measures shall be taken to provide for the emergence of green cover within 6 weeks of the application from a sown crop or from natural regeneration.

(5) Where green cover is provided for in compliance with this article, the cover shall not be removed by ploughing or by the use of a non-selective herbicide before 15 January unless a crop is sown within two weeks of its removal.

PART 5
GENERAL

General duty of occupier

22. (1) An occupier of a holding shall ensure compliance with the provisions of these Regulations in relation to that holding.

(2) An occupier of a holding shall, for the purposes of compliance with these Regulations, have regard to any advice or guidelines which may be issued from time to time for the purposes of these Regulations by the Minister, the Minister for Agriculture and Food or the Agency.

Keeping of records by occupier

23. (1) With effect from 1 August 2006, records shall be maintained for each holding which shall indicate–

    (a)   total area of the holding,
    (b)   net area of the holding,
    (c)   cropping regimes and their individual areas,
    (d)   livestock numbers and type,

(e)   an estimation of the annual fertiliser requirement for the holding and a copy of any Nutrient Management Plan prepared in relation to the holding,

(f)   quantities and types of chemical fertilisers moved on to or off the holding, including opening stock, records of purchase and closing stock,

(g)   livestock manure and other organic fertilisers moved on to or off the holding including quantities, type, dates and details of exporters and importers, as the case may be,

(h)   the results of any soil tests carried out in relation to the holding,

(i)   the nature and capacity of facilities on the holding for the storage of livestock manure and other organic fertilisers, soiled water and effluents from dungsteads, farmyard manure pits or silage pits including an assessment of compliance with Articles 8 to 13,

(j)   the quantities and types of concentrated feedstuff fed to grazing livestock on the holding, and

(k)   the location of any abstraction point of water used for human consumption from any surface watercourse, borehole, spring or well.

(2) Where fertiliser is used on a holding and a certificate of the type mentioned in Article 15 or 20 was issued in relation to that fertiliser in accordance with Article 32, a copy of the certificate shall be retained and be available for inspection on the holding for a period of not less than five years from the expiry of validity of the certificate.

(3) Records shall be prepared for each calendar year by 31 March of the following year and shall be retained for a period of not less than five years.

False or misleading information

24. A person shall not compile information which is false or misleading to a material extent or furnish any such information in any notice or other document for the purposes of these Regulations.

Authorised person

25. (1) In this article, "authorised person" means –

(a)   a person who is an authorised person for the purposes of section 28 of the Local Government (Water Pollution) Act 1977 (No. 1 of 1977), or

(b)   a person appointed under sub-article (12) to be an authorised person for the purposes of these Regulations.

(2) An authorised person may for any purpose connected with these Regulations–

    (a)   enter and inspect any premises for the purposes of performing a function under these Regulations or of obtaining any information which he or she may require for such purposes,

    (b)   at all reasonable times, or at any time if he or she has reasonable grounds for believing that there is or may be a risk to the environment, or that an offence under these Regulations is being or is about to be committed, arising from the carrying on of an activity at a premises, enter any premises and bring onto those premises such other persons (including a member of the Gárda Síochána) or equipment as he or she may consider necessary, or

    (c)   at any time if he or she has reasonable grounds for suspecting there may be a risk to the environment, or that an offence under these Regulations is being or is about to be committed, involving the use of any vehicle halt and board the vehicle and require the driver of the vehicle to take it to a place designated by the authorised person, and such a vehicle may be detained at that place by the authorised person for such period as he or she may consider necessary.

(3) An authorised person shall not enter into a private dwelling under this article unless one of the following conditions applies –

    (a)   the entry is effected with the consent of the occupier,

    (b)   the authorised person has given the occupier not less than 24 hours notice in writing of the intended entry, or

    (c)   the entry is authorised by a warrant issued under sub-article (7).

(4) Whenever an authorised person enters any premises or boards any vehicle, under this article, he or she may –

    a.   take photographs and carry out inspections, record information on data loggers, make tape, electrical, video or other recordings,

    b.   carry out tests and make copies of documents (including records kept in electronic form) found therein and take samples,

    c.   monitor any effluent, including trade effluent or other matter, which is contained in or discharged from a premises,

    d.   carry out surveys, take levels, make excavations and carry out examinations of depth and nature of subsoil,

    e.   require that the premises or vehicle or any part of the

premises or anything in the premises or vehicle shall be left
undisturbed for a specified period,

f. require information from an occupier of the premises of
any occupant of the vehicle or any person employed on the
premises or any other person on the premises,

g. require the production of, or inspect, records (including
records held in electronic form) or documents, or take copies
of or extracts from any records or documents, and

h. remove and retain documents and records (including
documents held in electronic form) for such period as may
be reasonable for further examination

which the authorised person, having regard to all the
circumstances, considers necessary for the purposes of exercising
any function under these Regulations.

(5) (a) An authorised person who, having entered any premises or
boarded any vehicle pursuant to these Regulations, considers
that a risk, to the environment arises from the carrying on
of an activity at the premises or involving the use of the
vehicle, may direct the owner or occupier of the premises
or the driver of the vehicle to take such measures as are
considered by that authorised person to be necessary to
remove that risk.

(b) If the owner, occupier or driver referred to in paragraph (a)
fails to comply with a direction of an authorised person
under this subsection, the authorised person may do all
things as are necessary to ensure that the measures required
under the direction are carried out and the costs incurred
by him or her in doing any such thing shall be recoverable
from the owner or occupier by him or her, or the person by
whom he or she was appointed.

(6) A person shall not –

(a) refuse to allow an authorised person to enter any premises
or board any vehicle or to bring any person or equipment
with him or her in the exercise of his or her powers,

(b) obstruct or impede an authorised person in the exercise of
any of his or her powers,

(c) give to an authorised person information which is to his or
her knowledge false or misleading in a material respect, or

(d) fail or refuse to comply with any direction or requirement
of an authorised person.

(7) (a) Where an authorised person in the exercise of his or her
powers under this article is prevented from entering any

premises, or if the authorised person has reason to believe that evidence related to a suspected offence under these Regulations may be present in any premises and that the evidence may be removed therefrom or destroyed, or if the authorised person has reason to believe that there is a significant immediate risk to the environment, the authorised person or the person by whom he or she was appointed may apply to the District Court for a warrant under this article authorising the entry by the authorised person onto or into the premises.

(b) If, on application being made to the District Court under this article, the District Court is satisfied, on the sworn information of the authorised person that he or she has been prevented from entering a premises, the Court may issue a warrant authorising that person, accompanied, if the Court deems it appropriate by another authorised person or a member of the Garda Síochána, as may be specified in the warrant, at any time or times within one month from the date of the issue of the warrant, on production if so requested of the warrant, to enter, if need be by force, the premises concerned and exercise the powers referred to in sub-article (4) or (5).

(8) An authorised person may, in the exercise of any power conferred on him or her by these Regulations involving the bringing of any vehicle to any place, or where he or she anticipates any obstruction in the exercise of any other power conferred on him or her by these Regulations, request a member of the Garda Siochána to assist him or her in the exercise of such a power and any member of the Garda Síochána to whom he or she makes such a request shall comply with this request.

(9) Any certificate or other evidence given, or to be given, in respect of any test, examination or analysis of any sample shall, in relation to that sample, be evidence, without further proof, of the result of the test, examination or analysis unless the contrary is shown.

(10) When exercising any power conferred on him or her by these Regulations an authorised person shall, if requested by any person affected, produce a certificate or other evidence of his or her appointment as an authorised person.

(11) Where a member of the Garda Siochana has reasonable cause to suspect that a person has committed an offence under these Regulations the member may without warrant arrest the person.

(12) A person may be appointed as an authorised person for the purposes of these Regulations by the Minister, the Minister for Agriculture and Food or the Agency.

(13) In this article "premises" includes land whether or not there are any structures on the land.

Offences

26. (1) A person who contravenes a provision of Parts 2 to 5 of these Regulations is guilty of an offence and shall be liable on summary conviction to a fine not exceeding €3,000 or to imprisonment for a term not exceeding six months or, at the discretion of the court, to both such fine and such imprisonment.

(2) Where an offence under these Regulations has been committed by a body corporate and it is proved to have been so committed with the consent or connivance of or to be attributable to any neglect on the part of any person who, when the offence was committed, was a director, manager, secretary or other officer of the body corporate, or a person purporting to act in any such capacity, that person, as well as the body corporate, is guilty of an offence and liable to be proceeded against and punished as if guilty of the first-mentioned offence.

(3) Where the affairs of a body corporate or unincorporated body are managed by its members, sub-article (2) shall apply to the acts and defaults of a member in connection with the functions of management as if such a member were a director or manager of the body.

(4) A prosecution for an offence under these Regulations may be taken by a local authority or the Agency.

(5) A prosecution for an offence may be taken by a local authority whether or not the offence is committed in the functional area of the authority.

(6) Where a court imposes a fine or affirms or varies a fine imposed by another court for an offence under these Regulations, prosecuted by the Agency or a local authority, it shall, on the application of the Agency or local authority concerned (made before the time of such imposition, affirmation or variation), provide by order for the payment of the amount of the fine to the Agency or local authority, as the case may be, and such payment may be enforced by the Agency or local authority, as the case may be, as if it were due to it on foot of a decree or order made by the court in civil proceedings.

(7) Where a person is convicted of an offence under these Regulations the court shall, unless it is satisfied that there are special and substantial reasons for not so doing, order the person to pay to the Agency or local authority concerned the costs and expenses, measured by the court, reasonably incurred by the Agency or local authority in relation to the investigation, detection and prosecution of the offence, including costs incurred in the taking of samples, the carrying out of tests, examinations and analyses and in respect of the remuneration and other expenses of employees, consultants and advisers.

PART 6
FUNCTIONS OF PUBLIC AUTHORITIES

Minister for Agriculture and Food

27. (1) The Minister for Agriculture and Food shall carry out, or cause to be carried out, such monitoring and evaluation programmes in relation to farm practices as may be necessary to determine the effectiveness of measures being

taken in accordance with these Regulations.

(2) The Minister for Agriculture and Food shall, in relation to each year, make the overall results of monitoring and evaluations carried out in accordance with sub-article (1) available to the Agency, to the Minister and, on request, to a local authority.

(3) The Minister for Agriculture and Food shall prepare and keep updated a register of all holdings and shall, on request, make a copy of the register available to the Agency or a local authority.

Making and review of action programme by the Minister

28. (1) The Minister shall, following consultation with the Minister for Agriculture and Food and other interested parties in accordance with this article, prepare and publish not later than 30 June 2009 and every four years thereafter, a programme of measures (hereafter in this article referred to as "an action programme") for the protection of waters against pollution from agriculture.

(2) An action programme required by sub-article (1) shall include all such measures as are necessary for the purposes of Article 5 of the Nitrates Directive and shall contain a review of the action programme most recently made for those purposes and of such additional measures and reinforced actions as may have been taken.

(3) The Minister shall ensure that all interested parties are given early and effective opportunities to participate in the preparation, review and revision of an action programme required by this article and for this purpose shall–

      (a)   inform interested parties by public notices or other appropriate means including electronic media, in relation to any proposals for the preparation, review or revision of an action programme,

      (b)   make available to interested parties information in relation to the proposals referred to in paragraph (a) including information about the right to participate in decision-making in relation to those proposals,

      (c)   provide an opportunity for comment by interested parties before any decision is made on the establishment, review or revision of an action programme,

      (d)   in making any such decision, take due account of the comments made by interested parties and the results of the public participation, and

      (e)   having examined any comments made by interested parties, make reasonable efforts to inform those parties of the decisions taken and the reasons and considerations on which those decisions are based, including information on the public participation process.

(4) The Minister shall ensure that such reasonable time is allowed as is sufficient

to enable interested parties to participate effectively.

(5) Where the Minister publishes any information in accordance with this article, the Minister shall–

    (a)   do so in such manner as the Minister considers appropriate for the purpose of bringing that information to the attention of the public, and

    (b)   make copies of that information accessible to interested parties free of charge through a website or otherwise.

(6) The Minister shall specify by way of public notice on a website or otherwise the detailed arrangements made to enable public participation in the preparation, review or revision of an action programme, including–

    (a)   the address to which comments in relation to those proposals may be submitted, and

    (b)   the date by which such comments should be received.

(7) In this article "interested parties" includes persons who -

    (a)   are carrying on any business which relies upon the water environment or which is affected, or likely to be affected, by the action programme, or

    (b)   are carrying on any activities which have or are likely to have an impact on water status, or

    (c)   have an interest in the protection of the water environment whether as users of the water environment or otherwise.

Agency

29. (1) The Agency shall prepare at four-yearly intervals a report in accordance with Article 10 of the Nitrates Directive and shall submit such report to the Minister.

(2) The Agency shall undertake a review of progress made in implementing these Regulations and shall submit a report to the Minister by 31 December 2008 and every four years thereafter with the results of that review and with recommendations as to such additional measures, if any, as appear to be necessary to prevent and reduce water pollution from agricultural sources.

(3) In preparing the reports required under sub-articles (1) and (2) the Agency shall consult with the Department of Agriculture and Food and the co-ordinating local authority in each river basin district, and such other persons as it considers appropriate.

(4) The Department of Agriculture and Food and the relevant local authorities shall provide the Agency with such information appropriate to their functions as may be requested by the Agency for the purposes of these Regulations.

(5) Each monitoring programme prepared by the Agency for the purposes of article 10 of European Communities (Water Policy) Regulations, 2003 (S.I. No. 722 of 2003) shall include provision for such monitoring as is necessary for the purposes of these Regulations.

(6) The Agency may make recommendations and give directions to a local authority in relation to the monitoring and inspections to be carried out, or other measures to be taken, by the authority for the purposes of these Regulations.

Local authorities

30. (1) A local authority shall carry out, or cause to be carried out, such monitoring of surface waters and groundwaters at selected measuring points within its functional area as makes it possible to establish the extent of pollution in the waters from agricultural sources and to determine trends in the occurrence and extent of such pollution.

(2) A local authority shall carry out or cause to be carried out such inspections of farm holdings as is necessary for the purposes of these Regulations and shall aim to co-ordinate its inspection activities with inspections carried out by other public authorities.

(3) For the purposes of sub-article (2) a local authority shall aim to develop co-ordination arrangements with other public authorities with a view to promoting consistency of approach in inspection procedures and administrative efficiencies between public authorities and to avoiding any unnecessary duplication of administrative procedures and shall have regard to any inspection protocol which may be developed by the Minister, following consultation with the Minister for Agriculture and Food.

(4) A local authority shall, in the exercise of its functions for the purposes of these Regulations–

    (a)   consult to such extent as it considers appropriate with the Minister, the Minister for Agriculture and Food, the Agency, the co-ordinating local authority in the relevant river basin district and such other persons as it considers appropriate, and

    (b)   have regard to any recommendations made, and comply with any direction given, to the authority by the Agency in accordance with Article 29.

(5) A local authority may furnish to the Department of Agriculture and Food and such other persons as it considers appropriate a report of an inspection or inspections carried out for the purposes of these Regulations.

(6) A local authority shall maintain a register of prior investigations carried out, and distances specified, for the purposes of Article 17(5).

Compliance with Data Protection Acts

31. The provision of information by a local authority, the Agency or the Minister for Agriculture and Food in accordance with Article 27, 29 or 30 of these Regulations shall not be a breach of the Data Protection Acts, 1988 and 2003.

Certificate in relation to nutrient content of fertiliser

32. (1) A certificate of the type specified in Article 15 or 20 may be issued by a competent authority where the authority is satisfied that the nutrient content of the fertiliser in question has been assessed on the basis of appropriate methodologies based on net farm balance and is as specified in the certificate.

(2) A certificate issued under this article shall be valid for such period, not exceeding twelve months, as shall be specified in the certificate.

(3) In this article "competent authority" means –

    (a)   the Agency in relation to fertiliser arising in an activity in relation to which there is in force a licence under Part IV of the Act of 1992, and

    (b)   the Minister for Agriculture and Food in relation to any other fertiliser.

(4) Notice of the methodologies used for the purposes of sub-article (1) shall be notified to the European Commission by the competent authority.

Exemption for exceptional circumstances for research

33. (1) A temporary exemption from a requirement of these Regulations may be granted to a person by the Agency or the Minister for Agriculture and Food in the case of exceptional circumstances relating to research.

(2) A temporary exemption for the purposes of sub-article (1) shall be granted by way of certificate issued to a person by the Agency or the Minister for Agriculture and Food and shall be subject to such conditions, if any, as are specified in the certificate.

(3) A certificate issued for the purposes of this article shall specify the nature, extent and duration of the exemption to which the certificate relates and a copy of the certificate shall be sent as soon as may be to the relevant local authority.

Transitional provisions

34. (1) A holding on which the application of fertilisers is carried out in accordance with a nutrient management plan approved on or before 1 December 2006 for the purposes of the Rural Environmental Protection Scheme shall be deemed to be compliant with the requirements of Article 16 for the duration of that plan.

(2) Notwithstanding Articles 16 and 26, the application of nitrogen or

phosphorus to land at any time prior to 30 October 2007 in quantities exceeding those prescribed by Article 16 shall not be an offence for the purposes of Article 16 in case where the nitrogen or phosphorus arises from an activity in relation to which there was in force on 30 April 2006 a licence under Part IV of the Act of 1992.

(3) Notwithstanding Articles 16 and 26 and sub-article (2), the application to land prior to 1 January 2011 of phosphorus in excess of the quantities prescribed by Article 16 shall not be an offence for the purposes of Article 16 in a case where –

(a) the excess arises from the application of spent mushroom compost or manure produced by pigs or poultry,

(b) such compost or manure, as the case may be, is produced on a holding on which, on the making of these Regulations, activities were being carried on which gave rise to spent mushroom compost or manure from pigs or poultry and there has not been an increase in the scale of such activities on the holding subsequent to the making of these Regulations, and

(c) the occupier of the holding on which the phosphorus is applied to land holds records which demonstrate compliance with paragraphs (a) and (b).

SCHEDULE 1

Article 3

SOIL TEST

A soil test refers to the results of an analysis of a soil sample carried out by a soil-testing laboratory approved by Department of Agriculture and Food.

The analysis for Phosphorus and, where appropriate, organic matter content and the taking of soil samples shall be carried out in accordance with the procedures below.

ANALYSIS FOR PHOSPHORUS

The Morgan's extractable P test as detailed below shall be used to determine the Soil P Index.

PREPARATION OF SOIL SAMPLE

The soil shall be dried at 40ºC for at least 24 hours (longer if necessary to ensure complete drying) in a forced draught oven with moisture extraction facilities. It shall then be sieved through a 2 mm mesh screen to remove stones and plant debris. After thorough mixing, it shall be sub-divided to obtain a representative sample. Where large samples are received at the laboratory, the entire sample shall be dried and sieved prior to sub-sampling for analysis.

MORGAN'S EXTRACTING SOLUTION

Constituents:- 1,400 ml of 40% NaOH in approximately 15 litres of water. Add 1,440 ml of Glacial Acetic Acid. Make up to 20 litres with water and adjust pH to 4.8. The pH of the solution must be checked regularly and adjusted as necessary before use. A volume ratio of one part sieved soil to five parts of solution must be used, e.g. 6 ml of the prepared soil sample is extracted with a 30 ml volume of Morgan's Extracting Solution. The sample shall be shaken for 30 minutes to get a suitable mix and permit intended reaction, after which it is filtered through a No 2 Whatman filter paper into vials for analysis. The filtered extract shall be analysed using standard laboratory techniques.

Results shall be reported in mg per litre.

Analysis of organic matter

Organic Matter content shall be determined by loss on ignition.

> Place a quantity of the prepared soil sample in an oven for 16 hours at 105 °C. Remove and cool in a desiccator. Put approximately 4g of this soil into a pre-weighed crucible and determine the weight of the soil (initial weight). Place in a muffle furnace at 500°C for 16 hours for ashing. Remove the crucible, cool in a desiccator and determine the weight of the ash (final weight).

> The organic matter of the soil is the difference in weight between the initial and final weights expressed as a percentage of the initial weight.

SOIL SAMPLING PROCEDURE

The soil sample shall be taken in accordance with the procedure as specified below:

a) The sampling area shall not exceed 4 hectares. Exceptionally, where soil types and cropping of lands were similar during the previous five years, a sample area of up to 12 hectares shall be deemed acceptable.

b) Separate samples shall be taken from areas that are different

in soil type, previous cropping history, slope, drainage or
persistent poor yields.

c)   Any unusual spots such as old fences, ditches, drinking
troughs, dung or urine patches or where fertiliser or lime
has been heaped or spilled shall be avoided.

d)   A field shall not be sampled for phosphorus until 3 months
after the last application of any fertiliser containing this
nutrient (chemical or organic).

e)   The sampling pattern shown in the figure below shall be
followed. A soil core shall be taken to the full 100 mm depth.
20 cores shall be taken from the sampling area and placed
in the soil container to make up the sample. Ensure the
container is full of soil.

f)   The field and sample numbers shall be written/attached onto
the soil container.

Figure 1: Sampling pattern

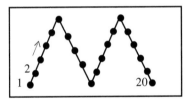

SCHEDULE 2

CRITERIA AS TO STORAGE CAPACITY AND NUTRIENT MANAGEMENT

Article 7

Table 1 Slurry storage capacity required for sows and pigs

Unit type	m³/week[1]				
Water:meal ratio changing for finishers only	2.0:1	2.5:1	3.0:1	3.5:1	4.0:1
Breeding unit (per sow place)	-	-	-	-	0.174
Integrated unit (per sow place)	0.312	0.355	0.398	0.441	0.483
Finishing unit (per pig)	0.024	0.031	0.039	0.046	0.053

[1] *An additional 200mm freeboard must be provided in all covered tanks and 300mm freeboard in all uncovered tanks*
Allowance must also be made for net rainfall during the specified storage period for uncovered tanks.

Article 7

Table 2 Slurry storage capacity required for cattle, sheep and poultry

Livestock type	m³/week[1]
Dairy cow	0.33
Suckler cow	0.29
Cattle > 2 years	0.26
Cattle (18-24 months old)	0.26
Cattle (12-18 months old)	0.15
Cattle (6-12 months old)	0.15
Cattle (0-6 months old)	0.08
Lowland ewe	0.03
Mountain ewe	0.02
Lamb-finishing	0.01
Poultry - layers per 1000 birds (30% DM)	0.81

[1] An additional 200mm freeboard must be provided in all covered tanks and 300mm freeboard in all uncovered tanks. Allowance must also be made for net rainfall during the specified storage period for uncovered tanks.

Table 3 Storage capacity required for dungstead manure

Livestock type	Solid fraction (m³/week)	Seepage fraction (m³ week)[1]
Dairy cow	0.28	0.04
Suckler cow	0.25	0.03
Cattle > 2 years	0.23	0.02
Cattle (18-24 months old)	0.23	0.02
Cattle (12-18 months old)	0.13	0.01
Cattle (6-12 months old)	0.13	0.01
Cattle (0-6 months old)	0.07	0.01

[1] Allowance must also be made for net rainfall during the specified storage period for uncovered tanks.

Table 4 Average net rainfall during the specified storage period

County	Millimetres per week
Carlow	24
Cavan	27
Clare	32
Cork	37
Donegal	38
Dublin	17
Galway	34
Kerry	45
Kildare	18
Kilkenny	23
Laois	22
Leitrim	33
Limerick	26
Longford	23
Louth	20
Mayo	40
Meath	19

Monaghan	23
Offaly	20
Roscommon	26
Sligo	32
Tipperary	27
Waterford	31
Westmeath	21
Wexford	25
Wicklow	33

Article 8

Table 5 Storage capacity required for effluent produced by ensiled forage

Crop	Minimum storage requirement (m³/100 tonnes)	
	Short Term Storage[1]	Full Storage
Grass	7	21
Arable silage	7	21
Maize	4	10
Sugar beet tops	15	50

[1] Only permitted where a vacuum tanker or an irrigation system is available on the holding.

Table 6 Annual nutrient excretion rates for livestock

Livestock type	Total Nitrogen kg/year	Total Phosphorus kg/year
Dairy cow	85	13
Suckler cow	65	10
Cattle (0-1 year old)	24	3
Cattle (1-2 year old)	57	8
Cattle > 2 years	65	10
Mountain ewe & lambs	7	1
Lowland ewe & lambs	13	2
Mountain hogget	4	0.6
Lowland hogget	6	1
Goat	9	1
Horse (>3 years old)	50	9
Horse (2-3 years old)	44	8
Horse (1-2 years old)	36	6
Horse foal (< 1 year old)	25	3
Donkey/small pony	30	5
Deer (red) 6 months - 2 years	13	2
Deer (red) > 2 years	25	4
Deer (fallow) 6 months - 2 years	7	1
Deer (fallow) > 2 years	13	2
Deer (sika) 6 months - 2 years	6	1
Deer (sika) > 2 years	10	2
Breeding unit (per sow place)	35	8
Integrated unit (per sow place)	87	17
Finishing unit (per pig place)	9.2	1.7
Laying hen per bird place	0.56	0.12
Broiler per bird place	0.24	0.09
Turkey per bird place	1	0.4

Articles 15 and 20

Table 7 Amount of nutrient contained in 1m³ of slurry

Livestock type	Total Nitrogen (kg)	Total Phosphorus (kg)
Cattle	5.0	0.8
Pig	4.2	0.8
Sheep	10.2	1.5
Poultry - layers 30% DM	13.7	2.9
For the purposes of calculation, assume that 1m³ = 1000 litres = 1 tonne.		

Articles 15 and 20

Table 8 Amount of nutrients contained in 1 tonne of organic fertilisers other than slurry

Livestock type		Total Nitrogen (kg)	Total Phosphorus (kg)
Poultry manure	broilers/deep litter	11.0	6.0
	layers 55% dry matter	23.0	5.5
	Turkeys	28.0	13.8
Dungstead manure (cattle)		3.5	0.9
Farmyard manure		4.5	1.2
Spent mushroom compost		8.0	2.5
Sewage sludge		Total nitrogen & total phosphorus content per tonne shall be as declared by the supplier in accordance with the Waste Management (Use of Sewage Sludge in Agriculture) Regulations, 1998 to 2001 and any subsequent amendments thereto.	
Dairy processing residues and other products not listed above		Total nitrogen & total phosphorus content per tonne based on certified analysis shall be provided by the supplier	

Article 15

Table 9 Nutrient availability in fertilisers

Fertiliser	Availability[1] (%)			
	From Jan 1 2007	*From Jan 1 2008*	*From Jan 1 2010*	*From Jan 1 2007*
Chemical	*100*	*100*	*100*	*100*
Pig and poultry manure	*35*	*40*	*50*	*100*
Farmyard manure	*20*	*25*	*30*	*100*
Spent mushroom compost	*35*	*40*	*45*	*100*
Cattle and other livestock manure (including that produced on the holding)	*30*	*35*	*40*	*100*

	Nitrogen	Phosphorus

[1]Refers to year of application

Article 15

Table 10 Determining nitrogen index for tillage crops

Continuous tillage:- crops that follow short leys (1-4 years) or tillage crops			
Nitrogen Index			
Index 1	Index 2	Index 3	Index 4
Cereals	Sugar beet		
Maize	Fodder beet		
	Potatoes		
	Mangels		
	Kale		
	Oil Seed Rape Peas,		
	Beans		
	Leys (1-4 years)		
	grazed or cut and		
	grazed.		
	Swedes removed	Swedes grazed in situ	

	Any crop receiving		
	dressings of organic		
	fertiliser		
Vegetables receiving less than 200 kg/ha nitrogen	Vegetables receiving more than 200 kg/ha nitrogen		

Tillage crops that follow permanent pasture			
Index 1	Index 2	Index 3	Index 4
Any crop sown as the 5th or subsequent tillage crop following permanent pasture	Any crop sown as the 3rd or 4th tillage crop following permanent pasture. If original permanent pasture was cut only, use index 1	Any crop sown as the 1st or 2nd tillage crop following permanent pasture (see also Index 4). If original permanent pasture was cut only, use index 2	Any crop sown as the 1st or 2nd tillage crop following very good permanent pasture which was grazed only

Article 15

Table 11 Phosphorus index system

Soil phosphorus index	Soil phosphorus ranges (mg/l)	
	Grassland	Other crops
1	0.0 - 3.0	0.0 - 3.0
2	3.1 - 5.0	3.1 - 6.0
3	5.1 - 8.0	6.1- 10.0
4	> 8.0	>10.0

Table 12 Annual maximum fertilisation rates of available nitrogen on grassland

Grassland stocking rate[1] (kg/ha/year)	Available nitrogen[2] (kg/ha)
= 170	226
Grassland stocking rate greater than 170 kg/ha/year[3]	
171-210	306
211-250	279

[1] Total annual nitrogen (kg) excreted by grazing livestock averaged over the net grassland area (ha) (grazing and silage area). Stocking rate refers to grassland area only.

[2] The maximum nitrogen fertilisation of grassland shall not exceed that specified for stocking rates less than or equal to 170 kg/ha/year unless a minimum of 5% of the net area of the holding is used to grow crops other than grass.

[3] This table does not imply any departure from Article 20(1) which prohibits the application to land on a holding of livestock manure in amounts which exceed 170kg Nitrogen per hectare per year, including that deposited by the animals themselves.

Table 13 Annual maximum fertilisation rates of phosphorus on grassland

Grassland stocking rate[1] (kg/ha/year)	Phosphorus Index			
	1	2	3	4
	Available Phosphorus (kg/ha)[2, 3,]			
≤130	35	25	15	0
131 -170	39	29	19	0
Grassland stocking rate greater than 170 kg/ha/year [4, 5]				
171-210	44	34	24	0
211-250	49	39	29	0

1. Total annual nitrogen (kg) excreted by grazing livestock averaged over the net grassland area (grazing and silage area). Stocking rate refers to grassland area only.

2. The fertilisation rates for soils which have more than 20% organic matter shall not exceed the amounts permitted for Index 3 soils.

3. Manure produced by grazing livestock on a holding may be applied to Index 4 soils on that holding in a situation where there is a surplus of such manure remaining after the phosphorus fertilisation needs of all crops on soils at phosphorus indices 1, 2 or 3 on the holding have been met by the use only of such manure produced on the holding.

4. The maximum phosphorus fertilisation of grassland shall not exceed that specified for stocking rates less than or equal to 170 kg/ha/year unless a minimum of 5% of the net area of the holding is used to grow crops other than grass.

5. This table does not imply any departure from Article 20(1) which prohibits the application to land on a holding of livestock manure in amounts which exceed 170kg Nitrogen per hectare per year, including that deposited by the animals themselves.

Article 16

Table 14 Annual maximum fertilisation rates of available nitrogen on grassland (cut only, no grazing livestock on holding)

	Available nitrogen (kg/ha)
1st cut	125
Subsequent cuts	100
Hay	80

Article 16

Table 15 Annual maximum fertilisation rates of phosphorus on grassland (cut only, no grazing livestock on holding)

	Phosphorus Index			
	1	2	3	4
	Available Phosphorus (kg/ha) [1]			
First cut	40	30	20	0
Subsequent cuts	10	10	10	0

[1] The fertilisation rates for soils which have more than 20% organic matter shall not exceed the amounts permitted for Index 3 soils.

Table 16 Maximum fertilisation rates of nitrogen on tillage crops

Crop	Nitrogen Index			
	1	2	3	4
	Available Nitrogen (kg/ha)			
Winter Wheat[1]	190	140	100	60
Spring Wheat[1, 2]	140	110	75	40
Winter Barley[1]	160	135	100	60
Spring Barley[1]	135	100	75	40
Winter Oats[1]	145	120	85	45
Spring Oats[1])	110	90	60	30
Sugar Beet	195	155	120	80
Fodder Beet	195	155	120	80
Potatoes: Main crop	170	145	120	95
Potatoes: Early	155	130	105	80
Potatoes: Seed	155	130	105	80
Maize	180	140	110	75
Field Peas/Beans	0	0	0	0
Oilseed Rape	225	180	160	140
Linseed	75	50	35	20
Swedes/Turnips	90	70	40	20
Kale	150	130	100	70
Forage Rape	130	120	110	90

[1] Where proof of higher yields is available, an additional 20kg N/ha may be applied for each additional tonne above the following yields;

Winter Wheat - 9.0 tonnes/ha   Spring Wheat - 7.5 tonnes/ha
Winter Barley - 8.5 tonnes/ha   Spring Barley - 7.5 tonnes/ha
Winter Oats - 7.5 tonnes/ha   Spring Oats - 6.5 tonnes/ha

The higher yields shall be based on the best yield achieved in any of the three previous harvests, at 20% moisture content.

[2] Where milling wheat is grown under a contract to a purchaser of milling wheat an extra 30 kg N/ha may be applied

Table 17 Maximum fertilisation rates of phosphorus on tillage crops

Crop	Phosphorus Index			
	1	2	3	4
	Available Phosphorus (kg/ha) [1]			
Winter Wheat	45	35	25	0
Spring Wheat	45	35	25	0
Winter Barley	45	35	25	0
Spring Barley	45	35	25	0
Winter Oats	45	35	25	0
Spring Oats	45	35	25	0
Sugar Beet	70	55	40	20
Fodder Beet	70	55	40	20
Potatoes: Main crop	125	100	75	50
Potatoes: Early	125	115	100	50
Potatoes: Seed	125	115	100	85
Maize	70	50	40	0
Field Peas	40	25	20	0
Field Beans	50	40	20	0
Oil Seed Rape	35	30	20	0
Linseed	35	30	20	0
Swedes/Turnips	70	60	40	40
Kale	60	50	30	0
Forage Rape	40	30	20	0

[1] The fertilisation rates for soils which have more than 20% organic matter shall not exceed the amounts permitted for Index 3 soils.

Table 18 Maximum fertilisation rates of nitrogen on vegetable crops

Crop	Nitrogen Index				
					Maximum additional supplementation (Top dressing)
	1	2	3	4	
	Available Nitrogen (kg/ha)				
Asparagus (Establishment)	140	115	95	70	
Asparagus (After harvest))	100	100	100	100	
Broad Beans	0	0	0	0	
French Beans	90	85	75	70	
Beetroot	140	125	105	90	
Brussels Sprouts	120	115	105	100	180
Spring Cabbage	50	35	15	0	250
Other Cabbage	150	135	115	100	100
Broccoli	120	110	100	90	20
Cauliflower (Winter & Spring)	75	50	25	0	150
Cauliflower (Summer & Autumn)	120	80	40	0	120
Carrots	90	75	55	40	
Celery	120	85	65	50	180
Courgettes	140	125	105	90	
Leeks	100	90	80	70	100
Lettuce	100	90	80	70	50
Onions	70	60	50	40	70
Scallions	90	80	70	60	60
Parsley	100	80	60	40	150
Parsnip	100	85	70	50	50
Peas (Market)	0	0	0	0	
Rhubarb	100	90	80	70	200

Spinach	140	125	105	90	100
Swede (Horticultural)	70	45	25	0	
Swede (Transplanted crops)	80	52	29	0	

Article 16

Table 19 Maximum fertilisation rates of phosphorus on vegetable crops

	Phosphorus Index			
Crop	1	2	3	4
	Available Phosphorus (kg/ha) [1]			
Asparagus (Establishment)	40	25	15	10
Asparagus (Maintenance)	27	17	10	7
Broad Beans	60	45	35	20
French Beans	60	45	35	20
Beetroot	60	45	35	20
Brussels Sprouts	60	45	35	20
Spring Cabbage	60	45	35	20
Other Cabbage	60	45	35	20
Broccoli	60	45	35	20
Cauliflower (Winter & Spring)	60	45	35	20
Cauliflower (Autumn)	60	45	35	20
Carrots	60	45	35	20
Celery	88	65	55	28
Courgettes	60	45	35	20
Leeks	60	45	35	20
Lettuce	60	45	35	20
Onions	60	45	35	20
Scallions	60	45	35	20
Parsley	60	45	35	20
Parsnip	60	45	35	20
Peas (Market)	60	45	35	20

Rhubarb	60	45	35	20
Spinach	60	45	35	20
Swede	70	60	45	35

[1] The fertilisation rates for soils which have more than 20% organic matter shall not exceed the amounts permitted for Index 3 soils.

Article 16

Table 20 Annual maximum fertilisation rates of nitrogen on fruit/soft fruit crops

	Available Nitrogen (kg/ha)
Apples (Desert)	30
Apples (Culinary)	60
Pears	50
Cherries	70
Plums	70
Blackcurrants	80
Gooseberries	40
Raspberries	60
Strawberries	0
Redcurrants	60
Loganberries	50
Blackberries	50

Table 21 Annual maximum fertilisation rates of phosphorus on fruit/soft fruit crops

	Phosphorus Index			
	1	2	3	4
	Available Phosphorus (kg/ha) [1]			
Apples (Desert)	25	16	12	8
Apples (Culinary)	20	12	10	8
Pears	16	8	4	0
Cherries	16	8	4	0
Plums	16	8	4	0
Blackcurrants	20	16	12	8
Gooseberries	20	16	12	8
Raspberries	20	16	12	8
Strawberries	16	8	4	0
Redcurrants	20	16	12	8
Loganberries	20	16	12	8
Blackberries	20	16	12	8

[1] The fertilisation rates for soils which have more than 20% organic matter shall not exceed the amounts permitted for Index 3 soils.

SCHEDULE 3

Articles 9, 10, 12

STORAGE PERIODS FOR LIVESTOCK MANURE

1. The storage period specified for the purposes of Articles 9(2), 10(2) and 12 is-

    (a)   16 weeks in relation to holdings in counties Carlow, Cork, Dublin, Kildare, Kilkenny, Laois, Offaly, Tipperary, Waterford, Wexford and Wicklow;

    (b)   18 weeks in relation to holdings in counties Clare, Galway, Kerry, Limerick, Longford, Louth, Mayo, Meath, Roscommon, Sligo and Westmeath;

    (c)   20 weeks in relation to holdings in counties Donegal and Leitrim, and

(d) 22 weeks in relation to holdings in counties Cavan and Monaghan.

2. Where a holding lies partly in one county and partly in one or more other counties, the holding shall be deemed for the purposes of this Schedule to lie wholly within the county in relation to which the longest storage period is specified by paragraph 1.

SCHEDULE 4

Articles 13, 17 and 19

PERIODS WHEN APPLICATION OF FERTILISERS TO LAND IS PROHIBITED

1. In counties Carlow, Cork, Dublin, Kildare, Kilkenny, Laois, Offaly, Tipperary, Waterford, Wexford and Wicklow, the period during which the application of fertilisers to land is prohibited is the period from -

   (a) 15 September to 12 January in the case of the application of chemical fertiliser

   (b) 15 October to 12 January in the case of the application of organic fertiliser (other than farmyard manure)

   (c) 1 November to 12 January in the case of the application of farmyard manure.

2. In counties Clare, Galway, Kerry, Limerick, Longford, Louth, Mayo, Meath, Roscommon, Sligo and Westmeath, the period during which the application of fertilisers to land is prohibited is the period from -

   (a) 15 September to 15 January in the case of the application of chemical fertiliser

   (b) 15 October to 15 January in the case of the application of organic fertiliser (other than farmyard manure)

   (c) 1 November to 15 January in the case of the application of farmyard manure.

3. In counties Cavan, Donegal, Leitrim and Monaghan, the period during which the application of fertilisers to land is prohibited is the period from -

   (a) 15 September to 31 January in the case of the application of chemical fertiliser

   (b) 15 October to 31 January in the case of the application of organic fertiliser (other than farmyard manure)

   (c) 1 November to 31 January in the case of the application of farmyard manure.

Given under the Official Seal of the Minister for the
Environment, Heritage and Local Government this 18th day of
July 2006

DICK ROCHE

Minister for the Environment, Heritage and Local Government

Explanatory Note

These Regulations revoke, and re-enact with amendments, the European
Communities (Good Agricultural Practice for Protection of Waters) Regulations,
2005 (S.I. No. 788 of 2005). These Regulations come into effect generally on 1
August 2006 with later commencement dates for certain provisions.

These Regulations provide statutory support for good agricultural practice to
protect waters against pollution from agricultural sources and include measures
such as -

- set periods when land application of fertilisers is prohibited
- limits on the land application of fertilisers
- storage requirements for livestock manure, and
- monitoring of the effectiveness of the measures in terms of
  agricultural practice and impact on water quality.

The Regulations give further effect to several EU Directives including Directives
in relation to protection of waters against pollution from agricultural sources ("the
Nitrates Directive"), dangerous substances in water, waste management, protection
of groundwater, public participation in policy development and water policy (the
Water Framework Directive).

Index

C
Cattle, *see* **Animals**
Constitution, 148

D
Department of Environment,
　　73, 86
Department of Food and
　　Agriculture, 49, 50, 80,
　　81, 94, 96, 97, 128-130,
　　131, 136, 156-161, 181,
　　194, 204, 205, 207
　　guidelines of, 160
　　policy of, 45, 157

E
Environment, 78 *et seq.*, *see*
　　also **Planning** and **Teagasc**
　　Environmental Protection
　　　　Agency (EPA), 95, 96
　　eutrophication, 78
　　Integrated Pollution
　　　　Prevention Licence
　　　　(IPPL), 96
　　issues and, 103-108
　　Landscape Conservation
　　　　Area (LDA), 104
　　Natural Heritage Area, 105
　　nitrates, 78, 79, 80, 81
　　　　fertilisation rates, 91, 92
　　　　general obligations and,
　　　　　　80
　　　　increased limits, 92-94
　　　　offences, 95
　　　　phosphorous fertilisation
　　　　　　rates, 89-91
　　　　record keeping, 94
　　　　tillage, 92
　　organic fertiliser storage
　　　　capacity zones, 97
　　preservation orders, 107

Environment—*contd.*
　　REPS(Rural Environmental
　　　　Protection Scheme), 96
　　　　et seq.
　　Special Amenity Area Order
　　　　(SAAO), 105, 106
　　Special Areas of
　　　　Conservation (SACs),
　　　　104
　　Special Protection Area
　　　　(SPAs), 104
　　Teagasc, *see* **Teagasc**
　　Tree Preservation Order
　　　　(TPO), 107, *see also*
　　　　Trees
　　Water pollution, *see* **Water**
　　　　pollution

F
Fences, 162 *et seq.*, *see also*
　　Boundaries, Trees and
　　Walls
　　function of, 162
　　hedge and ditch rule, 165
　　obligation to, 163
　　ownership of ditches and,
　　　　163
Foot and Mouth, 128, 130,
　　131, 133, *see also* **Animals**
Forestry, 76, 77, *see also*
　　Planning law
　　planning and, 76, 77

M
Milk quotas, 41, 47
Minister for Food and
　　Agriculture, 130-136, 139,
　　141, 144, 145 *et seq.*, 181,
　　185, 187, 197, 201-206
Minister for the Environment,
　　Heritage and Local
　　Government, 68, 87, 99,
　　105, 106, 151, 184

Succession—*contd.*
    onus of proof and, 32-35
    time limits for claims of,

T

Teagasc, 49, 81, 82, 86, 88, 89, 91, 100, *see also* **Environment** and **Planning**
Trees, 176 *et seq., see also* **Boundaries, Fences** and **Walls**
    damages for injuries from over hanging branches of, 178, 179
    preservation orders (TPO), 107, 108

W

Walls, 163 *et seq., See also* **Boundaries, Fences** and **Trees**
    boundary, 173, 174
    easements and, 174
    party, 166 *et seq.*
      repair of, 173

Water pollution, 98 *et seq., see also* **Environment**
    civil liability for, 101, 102
    offences of, 98, 99, 100, 101
Wildlife, 104, 105, 109-111, *see also* **Animals**
Wills, *see also* **Succession**
    amending, 26-28
    executor,
      functions of, 28, 29
    intestacy, 35
      rules and, 35
    issue,
      definition of, 37, 38
    next of kin,
      definition of, 38, 39
    proving, 28
    probate, granting of, 28
    spouse,
      definition of, 36, 37
    testation,
      freedom of, 29
    valid, 21, 22
      formalities for, 23-25